WITHDRAWN

S0-AIW-599

Turn-of-the-Century
FASHION PATTERNS
and Tailoring Techniques

S. S. Gordon

With a New Introduction by
Kristina Harris

Yeshiva University Museum

DOVER PUBLICATIONS, INC.
Mineola, New York

TT
520
.G67
2000

Copyright

Copyright © 2000 by Dover Publications, Inc.
All rights reserved under Pan American and International Copyright Conventions.

Bibliographical Note

This Dover edition is an unabridged reprint of *The "Standard" Work on Cutting Ladies' Tailor-Made Garments*, first published by The Jno. J. Mitchell Co., New York, in 1901. A new Introduction has been written specially for this edition. The illustrations on pages 20, 26, 37, 41, 65, 109, 114, 123, and 127 have been added and are taken from the May 1899, March 1902, and July 1902 issues of *The Delineator Magazine*, published by The Butterick Publishing Company, New York; the February 1902 issue of *The Designer*, published by the Standard Fashion Company, New York, London, and Toronto; and *Spring and Summer Styles: Cloaks, Suits, Waists, Skirts, Season 1900*, published by Edward B. Grossman, Chicago.

Library of Congress Cataloging-in-Publication Data

Gordon, S. S.
    [Standard work on cutting ladies' tailor-made garments]
    Turn-of-the-century fashion patterns and tailoring techniques / S.S. Gordon ; with a new introduction by Kristina Harris.
        p. cm.
    Originally published: The standard work on cutting ladies' tailor-made garments. New York : Jno. J. Mitchell Co., 1901.
    Includes index.
    ISBN 0-486-41241-5 (pbk.)
    1. Tailoring (Women's)—United States. 2. Garment cutting—United States. 3. Dressmaking—United States—Patterns. I. Title.
TT520 .G67 2000
646.4'07—dc21
                                                                00-063872

Manufactured in the United States of America
Dover Publications, Inc., 31 East 2nd Street, Mineola, N.Y. 11501

INTRODUCTION TO THE DOVER EDITION

The Standard Work on Cutting was among the last books of its kind. Though garment cutting manuals had been published since the late 1500s and had attained wide popularity in the 19th century, by the time this 1901 volume was published, it was fast becoming obsolete. *The Standard Work* was by now well established (having first appeared in the last quarter of the 19th century), and additional volumes would continue to be published up through the 1910s. But by the early 1900s, books offering scaled patterns were hardly necessary. Tissue paper sewing patterns, which had first appeared in large numbers in 1863, were now widely available for home sewers and dressmakers.

Yet, for a time at least, professional tailors still favored volumes like this one, with detailed scaled patterns that were useful for more than just the very latest trends. *The Standard Work* contained basic patterns that could be easily adapted to individual figures and tastes, as well as to ever-changing styles. For example, an Eton jacket is featured in this 1901 edition, but the Eton-style jacket for women first appeared in the 1880s and would not go entirely out of style until the 'teens. Also, tailoring was considered a specialty quite apart from paper patterns and dressmaking; for at least two more decades, it was the rare dressmaker who would even touch anything that was supposed to be tailored.

The technique and craft of tailoring was originally used only for men's garments. Beginning in the early 1800s, tailoring was also applied to some women's clothing. This is not quite as remarkable as it might sound, however, since up until the 18th century, women's dresses—although not sewn in what we would call a "tailored" style—were made by male tailors. Professionals specializing in the making of dresses simply did not exist.

Dr. C.W. Cunnington, one of the first to seriously study historic fashion, remarked that the innovation of using the technique of tailoring on women's clothing in the early 1800s "marked a profound change in [women's] social status, and [was], in fact, the only really original idea contributed to feminine costume since the fourteenth century" (*The Art of English Costume*, 1948). These early tailored women's garments were riding habits; only gradually did other types of feminine sportswear and everyday wear become available in tailored styles.

Women's tailored garments were nearly the opposite of other clothes worn by women. The vast majority of 19th-century women's clothing was trimmed abundantly with laces, beading, feathers, ruffles, and all manner of fussy and impractical details. On the other hand, women's tailored clothes were largely unfussed; a little flat braid or tone-on-tone embroidery was usually their only trim, and their lines were generally free from ruffles and excess.

At first considered suitable only for certain times and places, women's tailored suits gradually became so popular that by the early 1900s they were practically a uniform for everyday wear. Women wore them for shopping, for walking, for traveling, for the country, for riding in motor-cars, for their jobs (if they had them), and for many sports, including riding horses, hiking, and bicycling.

Not everyone thought tailored women's garments were an advance in fashion, however. As early as 1854, one of America's most prominent fashion magazines complained that women sometimes "disgust" even themselves. They "affect to borrow [masculine] ideas and sentiments, nay, even at times . . . adopt parts of our dress . . . What [would] these ladies think if they were to meet a gentleman trotting on horseback . . . dressed in hunting costume and a transparent bonnet trimmed with feathers and flowers?"

In the 1870s, when the tailored look for women was beginning to really take hold, a writer for Butterick's *The Metropolitan* expressed horror at the idea that tailored clothes might soon be banished from women's wardrobes. "I remember when the first feeble attempts were made to resuscitate this . . . style in 1861–62," she wrote, agreeing that "the first attempts at [tailored] jackets were so clumsy as to discourage most ladies from wearing them. But," she continued, "as all perfection comes through experience, we did better in a few years."

The skill of the tailor was bought at a premium, however; an 1872 issue of *The Metropolitan* complained that the price of ready-made tailored suits "was often much more than double the cost of material and making," which meant suits fashioned of fabric costing but $4 a yard were marked up to $350 or even $400. "If imported," the editors reported, "five hundred dollars is a common price." According to *Demorest's* magazine, by 1883 prices had lowered considerably. One writer noted that "plain cloth tailor-made suits of the best quality cost from ninety to a hundred dollars, and consist of four pieces: skirt, tunic, habit bodice, and outside walking coat, made almost exactly like the frock-coat of a gentleman."

By the 1890s, when tailored women's suits had become so common there were at least several in every lady's wardrobe, ads for such well-known businesses as the National Cloak Company (which created suits to order) made the prices quoted by *The Metropolitan* seem even steeper; their ads proudly announced "Jackets, Blazers and Reefers from $3.60 up; Capes $3.00 and up; Reefer Suits and Blazer Suits $7.50 and up."

Perhaps the most important reason women's tailored suits were adopted so widely—and struck such a responsive chord with women—was because they were, quite simply, practical. They were not distinctly more comfortable, nor were they easier or more practical to *wear* than most other dresses. But they *were* decidedly more practical to *care* for. "There is a limited class of *elegantes* . . . who indulge in elaborate puffs and fluting and complicated furbelows without a thought of the labor entailed upon the laundress," *The Lady's Friend* said in 1872, noticeably avoiding the thought that "the laundress" might very well be the wearer herself. "But most ladies find it well worth while to consider carefully the . . . make and trimming of their summer dresses . . . Buff linen suits for common morning wear are [ready-] made in great quantities [with] bias bands and bias folds, and even double bias ruffles are recklessly run on to these suits with sewing machine celerity." These trims were difficult to care for, making what should have been a practical garment entirely impractical. "They are frequently washed," the magazine noted, "and the ironing of these cross-cut trimmings . . . involves hours of tedious labor for which there is not adequate recompense in appearance." How to make the suit serviceable again? To rectify such a "blunder," the magazine suggested that its readers should "run off the mistaken trimming as recklessly as it was run on."

For reasons of practicality, too, the tailored dress remained popular for traveling. "The tailor-made dresses maintain their supremacy for traveling and all useful purposes," the editors of *Demorest's* wrote in 1883. "The plain woolen costume has, indeed, become an institution which nothing can displace, and all that is needed is, that it shall be well made in the neat, close-fitting forms which are alone adapted to solid, sober materials." Those "rough" suitings, "formerly worn by gentlemen only," as *The Voice of Fashion* put it in 1890, were so different and so much more practical than what women were used to, that, combined with simplicity in style, the tailored dress had no competition.

Certainly when it came to equestrian riding habits, there was never any competition for the tailored dress. In the Victorian era, riding habits changed relatively little. The sleeves might be set on full and low in the 1830s, and tight and narrow in the 1880s, and various fashionable colors might come and go, but the style remained relatively the same. "The style now is as near perfection as may be," *Demorest's* concluded in the 1880s. "Nor is it of any great use to describe [riding habits] in detail, for those who ride seriously, and can afford to keep horses and grooms, can afford to get a riding-habit from a good tailor." The editors were mindful, however, that riding habit skirts "must also be full enough not to embarrass the rider in case of an emergency."

When the bicycle took hold of women's imaginations in the 1890s, tailors looked to riding habits for inspiration. The most popular style of biking outfit was a tight bodice worn with full trousers ending at the knee, concealed, at least in part, by a short skirt. The major difference in style between riding habits and bicycling suits was that the skirt was far shorter for bicycling; the trousers (fully hidden beneath long skirts in riding habits) were also far fuller. It is interesting to note that this edition of *The Standard Work* discusses no need for obtaining an inseam measurement for riding trousers, although today tailors would consider such a measurement indispensable. *The Standard Work* offers tailors—who were inevitably male—only one note about manners when measuring a lady: "The knee size can be estimated." Bicycling suits were also described by *The Delineator* in 1895 as being "appropriate for hunting or mountain climbing, in which case it should be accompanied by laced or buttoned shoes of russet leather having low, broad heels."

The Standard Work not only provided a service to tailors of the era, but to women of the early 1900s, who longed for easy-care, yet attractive day suits, and chic, but practical sports clothes. Tailored clothes for women provided "swell effects," as one 1900 suit catalog put it, effects that helped make sports an increasingly open field for females, gave women more mobility, and gave them more time to explore their world—appropriate clothing, in fact, for the launching of a new kind of womanhood in the 20th century.

Kristina Harris
2000

THE "STANDARD"

WORK ON CUTTING

Ladies' Tailor=Made Garments

A COMPLETE TREATISE

ON THE

Art and Science of Delineating

All Garments for Women

Made by Tailors

BY S. S. GORDON,

Instructor, Ladies' Department, "Mitchell" School of Cutting

PUBLISHERS:

THE JNO. J. MITCHELL CO.,
NEW YORK

1901

Entered according to Act of Congress, in the year 1901, by

THE JNO. J. MITCHELL CO.

In the Office of the Librarian of Congress at Washington, D. C.

INDEX.

PAGE

Title - - - - - - - - - - - - 1
Preface - - - - - - - - - - 6
Introduction - - - - - - - - - - 8

PART I.—MEASURING.

The Measures - - - - - - - - 10
Appliances for Measuring - - - - - - 11
Measuring (with illustrations) - - - - - 12

PART II.—THE SYSTEMS.

Drafting - - - - - - - - - 22
Seam Allowances - - - - - - - - 22
Plain, Close Fitting Basque or Waist.   Back and Shoulder Sections - 23
Plain, Close Fitting Basque or Waist. (concluded) Waist and Hip Sections 27
Close-Fitting Waist.   Two Underarmpieces - - - - 30
Low-Neck Waist - - - - - - - - 32
Tight-Fitting Jacket—Two Bust Darts - - - - 34
Tight-Fitting Jacket (concluded) - - - - - 38
Tight-Fitting Jacket—Single Bust Dart - - - - 42
Bolero or Zouave Jacket - - - - - - 44
Short Dart - - - - - - - - - 44
Double-Breasted Short Jacket.   Half-Tight Fronts - - - 46
Full-Box Fronts - - - - - - - - 48
The Position of the Side-seam - - - - - 48
Jackets with Full Skirts - - - - - - 50
Whole Backs - - - - - - - - 50
Loose-Fitting Sack Jacket - - - - - - 52
Tight-Fitting Jacket—Vest Effect - - - - 54
Double-Breasted Frock Coat - - - - - 56
Double-Breasted Frock Coat (concluded) - - - - 58
Cutaway Frock Coat - - - - - - 60
Eton Jacket - - - - - - - - 62
Single-Breasted Box Coat - - - - - - 66
Plain Sleeve - - - - - - - - 68
Plain Sleeve (concluded) - - - - - - 70

PAGE

Sleeve with Enlarged Top - - - - - - - 72
Sleeve with Enlarged Top (concluded) - - - - - 74
Dart Sleeves - - - - - - - - 76
Enlarged Sleeve (MEDIUM LEG-O-MUTTON) - - - 78
Enlarged Sleeve (FULL LEG-O-MUTTON) - - - - 80
Bell or Wing Sleeve - - - - - - - 82
Collars - - - - - - - - - 84
Plain and Ripple Collarettes - - - - - - 88
Broad Collars - - - - - - - - 90
Three-Quarter, or Military Cape - - - - - - 92
Half-Circle Cape - - - - - - - 94
Hood - - - - - - - - - 96
Collarette Hood - - - - - - - - 96
Small Waist and Large Front Hip - - - - - 98
Corpulent Forms - - - - - - - - 100
Spreading the Darts - - - - - - - 102
Variations in Front-of-Scye and Half-Back Widths - - - - 104
Variations for Front Hip - - - - - - 105
Single-Breasted No-Collar Vest - - - - - - 106
Single-Breasted Notch-Collar Vest - - - - - 110
Double-Breasted Vest, Creased Collar - - - - - 112
Double-Breasted Vest, Flat Collar - - - - - 112
Skirts - - - - - - - - - 115
General Notes on Skirts - - - - - - - 119
Five-Gored Skirt, Underfolding Box-Plait - - - - 120
Skirt. Double Underfolding Box Plait - - - - 122
Skirt. Box-Plait on each side of Center-Back Seam - - - 124
Skirt. Box Plait at Back Center and one each side - - - 126
Skirt. Outward Double Box-Plait, Round and Trained Lengths - - 128
Skirt. Habit Back - - - - - - - 128
Skirt with Flounce - - - - - - - 130
Tunic - - - - - - - - - 132
Circular Skirt - - - - - - - - 134
Skirt with Yoke - - - - - - - - 136
Divided Skirt. Bicycle - - - - - - - 138
Skirts. Variations of Front, Side and Back Lengths - - - 140
Skirts. Variations for Prominent Stomach - - - - 142
Cross-Saddle Riding Skirt - - - - - - 144
Equestrian Skirt (SIDE SADDLE) - - - - - - 146
Trousers - - - - - - - - - 150
Riding Breeches - - - - - - - - 152
Knee Breeches - - - - - - - - 154

PAGE

Knickerbockers - - - - - - - - 156
Bloomers - - - - - - - - - 158
Leggings - - - - - - - - - 160
Raglan Box Coat - - - - - - - 162
Raglan Sleeve - - - - - - - - 164
Plain Ulster - - - - - - - - 166
Three-Seam Coat - - - - - - - 168
Inverness - - - - - - - - 170
Opera Cloak - - - - - - - - 174
Allowance for Seams and Inlays - - - - 180
Laying Out - - - - - - - - 182
Table of Proportionate Measures - - - - 184

PREFACE.

A N enduring system of garment cutting must be founded upon principles applicable to all variations of the human form and the ever-changing vagaries of fashion. As there is, however, no unity of opinion concerning the relative value of proportions and measurements as applied to custom garment cutting, thoughtful cutters have, by the force of their experience, become a law to themselves. They are not hampered by any well-spun theory lacking an understandable reason; but recognize the value of all general methods, and assign to each its legitimate field of usefulness.

There are departments in cutting in which the conditions and requirements render measures wholly unnecessary. Here proportions form the basis of procedure and the data thus obtained are adequate to the end in view. Proportions determine the lengths and widths of the parts that are adapted to a large proportion of forms of any given height and circumference. They are the outgrowth of experience, but vary in different localities according to conditions of physical development. Nevertheless their field of usefulness is a broad one.

In *custom* cutting, the requirements and conditions are widely different from those which obtain in the wholesale trade. In the former there is presented an almost infinite variety of forms, the requirements of each of which must be adequately met by the methods employed. Proportions alone are therefore insufficient for the custom cutter. For every average quantity there are two extremes between which the average has been established. For this reason there will always be a necessity for a comprehensive measurement *of the parts* into which the height and circumference of the whole may be properly divided.

The value of both proportions and measurements depends upon their approximate correctness, without which there is no choice between them. A correct measure is preferable to a false proportion, and also to an average proportion, when the form is not within the prescribed limits of an average form. On the other hand an average proportion is more desirable and reliable than a false measure. It is folly to condemn either *per se*.

As the whole is greater than any part, so is a system of garment cutting which is alike applicable to all forms superior, for the needs of the custom cutter, to one applicable to a large number only. While it is true that very many of the divergencies in shape from that of an average form may be ascertained and accommodated at the first or the second try-on, experience demonstrates that they can be more readily ascertained at the outset by a proper measurement of each form as presented to the cutter. The original pattern can then be made more closely to conform to the requirements of the wearer, thus minimizing the changes at the try-on.

For this reason the author has endeavored in the preparation of this work, to present and expound correct principles for all sizes and forms, and to provide a method by which they can be successfully applied. He has not undertaken to construct a system by which the unskilled can, with the aid of a try-on, produce suitable garments for even a large proportion of forms, but to construct one which, used by skilful cutters, will greatly lessen the changes at the try-on, and make the art of garment cutting pleasant and profitable.

The author believes that the principles upon which this system has been built are the most scientific yet employed in garment cutting; but even a perfect system will not be a guarantee of success to the cutter who is deficient in those qualities necessary to its intelligent utilization. No system will ever be invented that will supply any one with an equivalent for brains, or enable him to be successful in garment cutting unless he was born with an aptitude for the trade.

That this work may prove an inspiration and a valuable helper to all engaged in the production of women's tailor-made garments is the sincere wish and expectation of

THE AUTHOR.

INTRODUCTION.

IT has been thought best not to introduce many current style effects in this treatise. They are too subject to change, and in any event would prove of little value to the student.

The principles herein expounded are correct and applicable to any and all of fashion's caprices.

Those who are familiar with other works on this subject will readily recognize in this work many new and useful ideas. These will be welcomed by progressive cutters as valuable acquisitions to the art.

PART I.

MEASURING.

THE MEASURES.

THE measures required for a waist, bodice or any tight fitting garment which closes at the throat are as follows :

1. Half-Back width.
2. Back Scye depth.
3. Length to natural waist.
4. Full Length.
5. Blade.
6. Front Scye depth.
7. Over-Shoulder.
8. Sleeve.   (Lengths to elbow and full length.)
9. Back-Waist.
10. Front Hip.
11. Bust.
12. Waist.
13. Hip.
14. Half-Size of Neck.
15. Length to brow of bust.
16. Front Waist length.
17. Front Length.
18. Depth of Neck-gorge.

All the measures except the hip should be taken over a waist, or a smooth fitting bodice.

APPLIANCES FOR MEASURING.

THE appliances required are :
1. An inch tape measure.
2. A piece of tailor's chalk freshly sharpened.
3. A sliding arm measuring square.
4. An elastic belt which can be fastened by a buckle. The belt should be about an inch wide. Or a strong cord may be used, to be tied closely around the waist. The purpose of the belt, or cord, is to define clearly the waist line, when measuring for a tight fitting waist, basque or jacket, or for a skirt. The lower edge of the belt must be adjusted around the waist *level* with the bottom of the waist at the sides.

MEASURING.

THE position of the Collar-Seam at the back of the neck can be fixed by the eye, and should be indicated by a light chalk mark, or pencil point. The Collar-Seam of the waist over which the measures are to be taken may be used as a guide, and the mark made as much above or below the seam as may be deemed proper.

Raise the arms of the client slightly and place the *fixed* arm of the measuring square under the right arm, and the *sliding* arm under the left. Then allow the arms to drop to the sides, and at the same time bring the sliding arm just fair against the side of the body. The position of the measuring square is shown on Figure 1. Press up lightly and equally under each arm, and observe whether the long arm (which is extended across the back), is *level*, or on an incline from one side to the other. If level, this will indicate that the right and left scye depths are equal. If not, make note of the degree of incline, as for example, " Right shoulder ½ inch low."

Next note the *width of the body*, as indicated by the figures on the top side of the measuring-square at the sliding arm (which for a 36 bust is about 11½ inches). Make a light mark at the center of the back (half of 11½), and call off ¼ inch more than half for

THE FIRST MEASURE,

which is the half-back width.

Having thus located a point on the back, central to the width of the body near the scye level, take position at the left of client, and, supporting the outer end of the sliding arm by the tips of the fingers of the left hand, bring the sliding arm to a *level* as shown on Figure 2. The long arm of the measuring square should rest lightly on the fingers of the right hand. *Do not press upwards more than just enough to bring the long arm of the square level with the bottom of the scye.* Then, pressing the square firmly against the back, let go of the brass arm, take position again at back of client, hold the square in its position by the left hand, and with the right mark lightly with chalk or pencil point on the *top* side of the square at the middle of the back as shown on Figure 3. Remove the square.

Place the long arm of the measuring square across the back at the waist, each brass arm *close to the side at the bottom of the waist*. Bring the long arm *level with the waist length at the sides*, and mark lightly on the *under* side of the long arm at the center of the back as shown on Figure 4. Make a mark on the *under* side of the brass arm at the left side. Remove the square.

Put a pin crosswise on the left side, 5½ inches below the side waist length, and another the same distance below the waist length at the center-of-back.

THE SECOND MEASURE.

BACK SCYE DEPTH.

Place the end of the tape measure at the mark made for collar seam, and measure to the mark made at the scye depth.

Figure 1.

Figure 2.

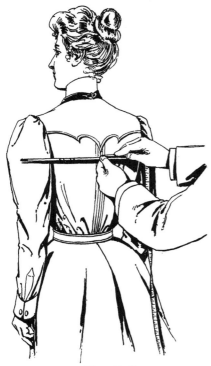

Figure 3.

Figure 4.

THE THIRD MEASURE.

LENGTH TO NATURAL WAIST.

Still holding the end of the tape at the mark made for the collar-seam, measure to the mark made at the natural waist. It must be distinctly observed that the length to the natural waist is always taken to a point at the center of the back *level with the bottom of the waist at the side.* Quite frequently the actual waist length is greater at the center-of-back than it is at the sides. Any difference between the two should be noted as follows: "Natural waist length level with length at side [say] 15 inches, and length at the center-of-back [say] 15¾ inches."

THE FOURTH MEASURE.

LENGTH.

Still holding the end of the tape at the collar-seam, measure for the full length desired.

THE FIFTH MEASURE.

BLADE.

Take the sliding-arm measuring-square (the sliding arm being removed), extend the tape measure (which is attached at the angle at the fixed brass arm) along the fixed brass arm, and grasp both the arm and tape firmly by a full clasp of the right hand at the outer end of the brass arm. With the left hand draw the client's left arm away from the side of the body and bring the angle of the measuring-square up under the arm of client, the brass arm just touching the bottom of the arm-scye, and the long arm *close* against the front of the shoulder, as shown on Figure 5. The angle of the square must be allowed to find the natural point of juncture of arm and body, the square being held *only* in the right hand by the fixed brass arm, the left hand being employed in holding the arm of client away from the side of the body. When the angle of the square has been in this manner adjusted to the bottom and front of the scye, allow client's arm to fall naturally to the side of the body, and hold the square in its position by the left hand *at the hollow of the waist.* With the right hand extend the tape across the blade and take a fairly close, but not a tight measure, to the center of the back as shown on Figure 6.

THE SIXTH MEASURE.

FRONT-SCYE DEPTH.

Without removing the square from the position shown on Figure 6, and still holding it with the left hand, swing the tape with the right hand down and under the arm of client until you can grasp it between the second and third fingers of the left hand. The tape should be drawn sufficiently tight, so that the swivel, to which it is attached, will turn with it. Draw the tape toward the front with the fingers of the left hand, and with the right hand draw it up and over the left shoulder. A little practice will enable one to bring the tape to this position easily and quickly.

Figure 5.

Figure 6.

Figure 7.

Figure 8.

During this operation *do not let go of the measuring-square with the left hand, but carry the tape up over the shoulder with the right hand.* Observe particularly that the brass arm of the square *does not press up,* but barely touches the bottom of the scye. Now take an *easy* measure to the center-of-back at the collar-seam, as shown on Figure 7.

THE SEVENTH MEASURE.

OVER-SHOULDER.

Without removing the square from the position shown on Figure 7, bring the tape over the shoulder about two-thirds of the distance from the side of the neck to the outer shoulder, and take an *easy* measure in a direct line to the mark made at the scye-depth at the center-of-back, as shown on Figure 8.

THE EIGHTH MEASURE.

SLEEVE-LENGTHS.

Without removing the square note the underarm sleeve lengths to the elbow and the full length by the figures on the long arm of the measuring-square.

THE NINTH MEASURE.

BACK-WAIST.

The angle of the measuring-square is still held in position at the front and bottom of the scye..

Particular attention must now be given to bring the long arm of the square in as nearly an upright position as possible. The upper part must be pressed close against the front of the shoulder, as when the fifth, or blade, measure was taken, and the lower part moved forward or backward as may be necessary to bring the long arm into a perpendicular position. Then make a light mark with chalk or pencil point on the side of the body at the natural waist, and opposite the back edge of the square, as shown on Figure 9.

Also make a light mark at the back edge of the square on the side of the hip opposite the pin (5½ inches below the natural waist).

Remove the square; place the end of the tape measure at the point just located at the side of the waist, and take an easy measure directly across to the center of the back, as shown on Figure 10.

THE TENTH MEASURE.

FRONT-HIP.

As an aid to locate rightly the center of the body in front, place the tape-measure around the waist, bring the end to the center of the back, and note the full size around the waist, say 24 inches. Now make a mark at one-half the waist, 12 inches, at the waist line in front.

Figure 9.

Figure 10.

Figure 11.

Figure 12.

Place the end of the tape-measure at the point made at the side of the hip, and take an easy measure across the front-hip to the center-of-front directly under the mark made at the waist.

THE ELEVENTH MEASURE.

BUST.

This measure is taken over the largest part, the tape passing close up under the arms on a line towards the mark made for the back-scye depth as shown on Figure 11.   On slight forms this measure should be taken easy, and on stout forms fairly close, but not tight.

THE TWELFTH MEASURE.

WAIST.

This measure must be taken *close* over·the smallest part.

THE THIRTEENTH MEASURE.

HIP.

This measure must be taken 5½ inches below the natural waist, quite easy for all body garments and skirts, but fairly close for trousers, knickerbockers and such like garments.

THE FOURTEENTH MEASURE.

HALF SIZE OF NECK.

Place the end of the tape-measure at the collar-seam at the center-of-back, and measure close around on the line of the gorge to the center-of-neck in front, at the depth desired for front-of-gorge, as shown on Figure 12.

THE FIFTEENTH MEASURE.

LENGTH TO BROW OF BUST.

Without removing the end of the tape-measure from the center-of-back at the collar-seam, measure to a point ½ inch below the brow of bust.   The tape should be drawn midway between the center-of-front and front of scye.

THE SIXTEENTH MEASURE.

FRONT WAIST LENGTH.

The end of the tape-measure is still held at the center-of-back and collar-seam. From there measure in a direct line to the bottom of the waist at the center-of-front.

Figure 13.

THE SEVENTEENTH MEASURE.

FRONT LENGTH.

The end of the tape-measure is still held at the center-of-back and collar-seam. From there measure in a direct line to the full length desired at the center-of-front.

THE EIGHTEENTH MEASURE.

DEPTH OF GORGE.

Still holding the end of the tape-measure at the center-of-back and collar-seam, bring the tape with the right hand closely to the center-of-front on the waist-line. Hold the tape at the waist with the fingers of the right hand, release the end from the back of the neck and extend it up directly to the center-of-neck in front. Note the number of inches on the tape where it passes the gorge-line at the depth desired as shown on Figure 13.

The greatest care must be exercised when locating the several measuring points and when taking the measures. The student must become familiar by careful study with the foregoing instructions in measuring. Then, *practice* will soon enable him to determine with all-sufficient accuracy the lengths and widths of all of the parts, in their relations to each other.

Ladies' Suit
The Designer
February 1902

PART II.

THE SYSTEMS.

DRAFTING.

IN all of the following explanations, wherever the fractions ⅙, ¼, ⅓, ½, etc., are used, unless expressly stated otherwise, they are according to the several divisions of the half-bust, half-waist or half-hip found on the ordinary drafting square. As for example the distance between two given points may be given as ¼ waist, the waist being 24 inches. Find half of 24 which is 12, on the divisions of fourths. From this to the angle of the drafting square is ¼ waist or 3 inches for this size of waist. When it is said that from one point to another is one *full fourth* of the waist, the waist being 24 inches, then is meant one full fourth or 6 inches.

Take a 36 bust, one full half bust would be 18 inches. But ½ bust is the quantity on the drafting square between the angle and half of the bust 18, on the divisions of halves, viz., 9 inches.

SEAM ALLOWANCES.

ALL the drafts in this book are made to the measures as taken on the form unless explicitly stated otherwise. These represent the lengths and widths of the finished garment and its parts. *Therefore all seams must be allowed for when cutting the material.*

PLAIN CLOSE FITTING BASQUE OR WAIST.

BACK AND SHOULDER SECTIONS.

DIAGRAM I.

[NOTE.—I begin the illustrations and explanations of drafting women's garments with the plain close fitting basque, as the principles employed in drafting the basque underlie the construction of all close fitting body garments.]

The measures used for this diagram and for Diagram 2 are as follows:

5¾ half-back width.	9 front-hip.
7¼ back-scye depth.	36 bust.
15½ length to natural waist.	24 waist.
19 length.	42 hip.
10¼ blade.	7¼ half-size of neck.
11¼ front-scye depth.	13½ brow of bust.
15¾ over-shoulder.	19½ front-waist length.
6¼ back-waist.	6 depth of neck-gorge.

As this garment is to be worn next to the corset-cover, the blade and back-waist are each reduced ¼ inch, and the waist ½ inch, so that in drafting the blade will be 10, the back-waist 6, and the waist 23½ inches.

TO DRAFT.

Draw a straight line as from 1 to C.

From 1 to A is $\frac{1}{24}$ bust. A to B is the back-scye depth. A to C is the length to the natural waist. Square the cross lines from 1, B and C.

C to E is $\frac{1}{12}$ bust for sizes of 36 bust and under. When the bust is more than 36, C to E is 1½ inch. Draw a straight line from A to E. This establishes F.

F to G is ¼ inch less than the blade, *as the garment is to be worn next to the corset cover.*

G to H is ½ inch more than ⅙ bust.

F to 13 is one full half of bust, and 13 to I is ½ inch. Square up from H.

On the divisions of two-thirds on the drafting square, we find that the blade size used, viz., 10 inches, is opposite 15, which shows that the blade is equal to ⅔ of 30 bust. Now find 15 on the divisions of fourths, which is 3¾ inches for this draft. Place 15 on fourths at G and make a mark at the angle of the square as at J. Square up from J to establish K.

From 1 to L is one-half the quantity between G and J. It may be made more if desired, as $\frac{1}{8}$ bust, or $\frac{1}{4}$ inch less than $\frac{1}{8}$ bust. Draw a straight line from L to I.

K to M is $\frac{1}{16}$ bust, and G to 10 is the same.

F to S is the same as 1 to M. Connect M and S to establish 7.

From 7 to 8 is $\frac{1}{4}$ inch. Shape the back-scye from 8 to the bust line as represented.

Draw a guide line from 8 to a point half-way between E and 2. Make the width from 8 to 9 to style. On the diagram it is $\frac{1}{8}$ bust.

E to 2 is $\frac{3}{4}$ inch. It may be made a trifle more or less than $\frac{3}{4}$ inch according to style or taste. Shape the side-seam from 9 to 2 as represented.

G to N is the front-scye depth less the width of the top of the back A to L. Connect G and N to establish R.

Point 5 is half-way from A to B. Connect 5 and N.

Connect F and M to establish 6.

N to 14 is the same as L to 6.

F to 6 and G through R to 14 is the over-shoulder.

N to 11 is the same as L to 8.

Square up from 10 and finish the scye from 11 to the bust line as represented.

Make the sleeve notch at front of scye $\frac{1}{12}$ bust above 10.

Square forward from N. N to O is $\frac{1}{2}$ inch less than $\frac{1}{6}$ bust. Draw a straight line from O through 13 to establish P.

N to 12 is $\frac{1}{2}$ inch less than $\frac{1}{4}$ bust for the average form.

For all garments which close at the throat, and are worn next to the corset-cover, proceed in the following manner to establish O: Take the width of the top of the back, A to L. Place this at N and extend the tape measure in a direct line to the front waist, as to P. Hold the tape at P, release it from N and extend the end up the center-of-front line. Now cast a short sweep at or near 12 according to the measure taken for depth of gorge, 6 inches for this draft. Then apply the half-neck measure, less $\frac{1}{2}$ inch, from A to L and N to the sweep for depth of gorge.

Shape the center-of-front line from 12 passing $\frac{1}{8}$ inch forward of 13 through 25, which is $\frac{1}{4}$ inch back of P.

NOTE.—The method of obtaining the half-back width opposite 9, as above explained, is only used when drafting a pattern with that part in proportion to the blade size. In custom cutting it will serve as a guide in obtaining the half-back width, but the measure should be applied as taken on the form in the following manner:

From 1 to M is the half-back width. F to S is the same as 1 to M. Connect M and S to establish 7. Then proceed as already explained.

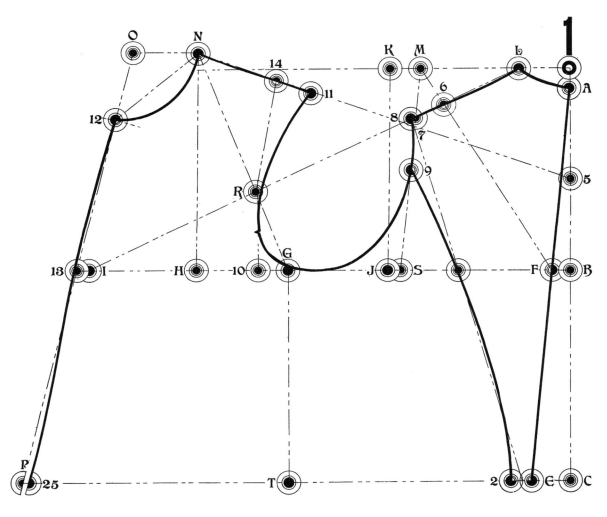

DIAGRAM 1.

Man-Tailored Suit
Edward B. Grossman & Co.
1900 catalog

Walking Toilette
The Delineator
March 1902

Eton Jacket Suit
Edward B. Grossman & Co.
1900 catalog

Plain, Close-Fitting Basque or Waist.

(Concluded.)

WAIST AND HIP SECTIONS.

DIAGRAM 2.

Connect 9 and the notch at front of scye. From 9 to 0 is ¼ inch.

Square down from G to establish T and Q. *Point 19 on this draft is ½ inch less than half-way from 10 to J (Diagram 1). For the small sizes it may be placed nearer to G as shown on Diagram 3, and for large sizes, when only one underarm piece is desired, it may be placed half-way from 10 to J.*

T to 17 is ½ inch more than G to 19. Draw a straight line from 19 through T to establish W.

T to U is ¼ inch less than the back-waist for all garments which are worn next to the corset cover.

U to E represents the *surplus through the back-waist* over the size required. This surplus is disposed of as follows : For this draft the back-waist surplus is 3¼ inches. About one-half of it, say 1½ inch is taken out between 16 and 18, distributed equally on each side of 17. One-half of the remainder, say ⅞ inch is taken out between the back and sidebody as from 2 to 14. From 14 to 15 is ¼ inch less than half-way from 14 to 16. The remaining ⅞ inch of back-waist surplus is now distributed equally on each side of 15.

From 19 to 20 is ¼ inch less than half-way from 19 to the side seam of the back. Draw a straight line through 20 and 15 to establish X.

It must be borne in mind that C (the point to which the length to the natural waist is taken) is level with the bottom of the waist at the sides. Frequently the length is greater at the center of back than it is at the sides. This should be noticed when the measures are taken, and a memorandum made of the extra length at the back as from C to S.

For this draft C to S is ¾ inch. Connect T and S.

U to V is ¼ inch less than one full half of waist. V to 25 represents the *front waist surplus.* This is disposed of by the darts as follows :

The width of the part from 25 to 23 may be made according to taste or style. On the diagram it is 1½ inch. From 23 to 26 is about ½ inch less than half of the front waist surplus. From 26 to 27 is 1 inch. From 27 to 29 is the remainder of the front waist surplus. Establish 24 half-way between 23 and 26, and 28 half-way between 27 and 29.

Divide the quantity between G and 13 into three equal parts. This establishes 21 and 22. Draw straight lines from a point ½ inch back of 21 through 24 to establish 34, and from 22 through 28 to establish 27.

From 22 to 31, for the average form, is ½ inch less than one-third of the distance between the bust and waist lines. *For custom work however, the position of the top of the darts is found by applying the 15th measure (length to brow of bust) as from A to L and N to 31.*

Draw a line from F through 31 to establish 30.

Draw guide lines from 30 to 23 and to 26, also from 31 to 27 and to 29.

N to 6 is the front-waist length less the width of the top of the back A to L.

Sweep back from 6 to the front of the first dart, pivoting at 12. Sweep across the dart, pivoting at 30. Extend the line across the tongue between the darts parallel with the original waist line. Sweep back across the second dart, pivoting at 31.

The hip line is always 5½ inches below the natural waist line, and is represented by the line which is squared across from C1.

Extend the center-of-front line to establish 32. Draw a line from 8 through the unlettered point just below 14 to the hip line to establish Y. Square down from 2 and E to establish 3 and 4. From 4 to 43 is 1 inch. Complete the back from E towards 43. Shape the sidebody from 0 through 14 to a point ¼ inch back of Y.

Q to Z is 1 inch less than the front hip. Z to 32 represents the *front hip surplus*, which must be taken out by the darts as follows: From 34 to 33 is ¼ inch less than from 23 to 24. From 37 to 36 is ¼ inch less than from 27 to 28. From 36 to 35 is ½ inch more than from 26 to 27, excepting for forms that are flat through the front hip, when it may be made the same as from 26 to 27.

Now deduct the quantity between 33 and 35 from that between Z and 32, and the remainder will be the quantity between 36 and 38.

Draw guide lines from 23 to 33, from 26 to 35, from 27 to 36, and from 29 to 38, and shape the darts as represented.

The spring over the hip at W and X is found in the following manner: Take the width from 3 to 43. Place this at Z and measure to the back edge of the sidebody, which is ¼ inch back of Y. For this draft, this measure is 18¾ inches. This is 2¼ inches less than half of the full hip size required as determined by the hip measure. This deficiency of 2¼ inches is added by overlapping the parts on each side of W and X as follows: About two-thirds of it or 1½ inch for this draft is distributed equally on each side of W, and the remaining ¾ inch equally on each side of X. This establishes 39, 40, 41 and 42. Draw the guide lines and shape the seams below 19 and 20 as represented.

Cast short sweeps for the back waist notches, first from 2 forward, pivoting at the unlettered disk above on the bust line, then across opposite 15, pivoting at 20, and from 17 pivoting at 19.

A to D is the length. Shape the bottom to taste or style. The line from 12 through 25 to 32 represents the center-of-front.

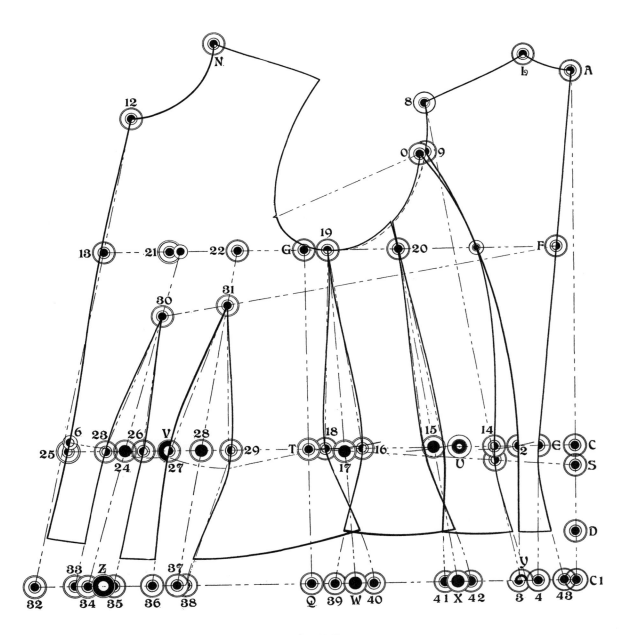

DIAGRAM 2.

CLOSE=FITTING WAIST.

Two Underarmpieces.

DIAGRAM 3.

THE measures used for the accompanying diagram are as follows : 8 back-scye depth, 16¼ length to natural waist, 18¼ length, 12 blade, 12¾ front-scye depth, 17½ over-shoulder, 8 back-waist, 10½ front-hip, 20¼ front-waist length, 23 front length, 42 bust, 30 waist, 49 hip.

The back and shoulder sections are drafted in the same manner as explained for Diagram 1.

The front-waist section is drafted in the same manner as explained for Diagram 2.

T to U is ¼ inch less than the back-waist measure for all garments that are worn next to the corset-cover.

U to E represents the *back-waist surplus* 3⅛ inches for this draft.   This surplus is disposed of as follows :

T to 23 is one-half of the back-waist surplus, say 1⅝ inch for this draft.   From 2 to 14 is one-fourth of the back-waist surplus, ¾ inch for this draft.   From 14 to 15 is ¼ inch less than one-third the distance from 14 to 23.   One-half of the remainder of back-waist surplus, ⅜ inch, is distributed equally on each side of 15. Half-way between 22 and 23 establish 16.   The remaining ⅜ inch of back-waist surplus is distributed equally on each side of 16.

Half-way between T and 23 establish 17.

G to 19 is ½ inch less than T to 17.

Draw a straight line from 19 through 17 to establish W.

Point 18 is one-third of the quantity between 24 and 19.

From 18 to 21 is ½ inch.

Draw a straight line through 21 and 15 to establish X1.

Point 20 is half-way between 19 and 21.

Draw a straight line from 20 through 16 to establish X.

To obtain the run of the lines below the waist-line, proceed in the same manner as explained for Diagram 2 with the following exception :

One-half of the quantity which is added at the hip line on Diagram 2 between 41 and 42, is distributed equally on each side of X, and the remainder equally on each side of X1.

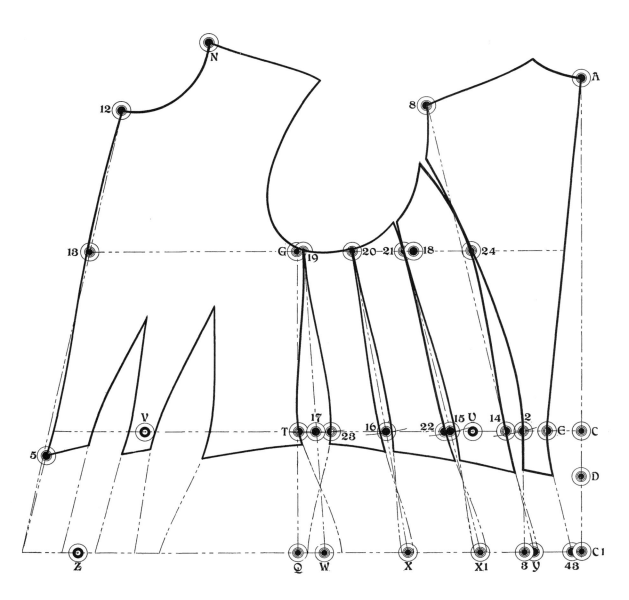

DIAGRAM 3.

LOW NECK WAIST.

––––––

DIAGRAM 4.

THE waist is drafted to the measures, and in the same manner as explained for the preceding diagram.

The pattern is then cut down on the front and back to within 2 inches, more or ess, of the bust-line in either of the three shapes represented, square, oval or straight, as may be desired.

For all dress waists two underarmpieces are preferable in order that a smooth fit may be obtained about the waist.

A ¼ inch V is usually taken out of the lining only, at the front on the bust line as represented.

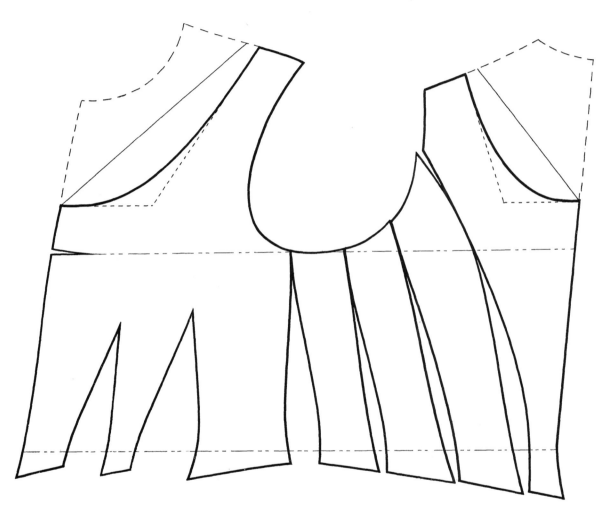

DIAGRAM 4.

TIGHT=FITTING JACKETS.

Two Bust Darts.

JACKETS are drafted on the same general principle as employed for the preceding diagrams. As a jacket, however, is worn *over* a waist or vest, the measures are applied to the draft as they are taken on the form without reduction of the blade, back-waist, or full-waist quantities (as explained for waists), and ½ inch is added to the full half of bust as from I to 13. From N to O and from N to 12 are each ½ inch more than as explained for waists, and the scye is sunk ¼ inch below the bust line.

DIAGRAM 5.

The measures used are as follows: 5¾ half-back width, 7¼ back-scye depth, 15½ length to natural waist, 32 length, 10¼ blade, 11¼ front-scye depth, 15¾ over-shoulder, 6¼ back-waist, 9 front hip, 36 bust, 24 waist, 42 hip, 13 brow of bust, 19½ front-waist length, 7¼ half size of neck, 6 depth of neck-gorge.

TO DRAFT.

Draw a straight line as 1 D. From 1 to A is $\frac{1}{24}$ bust. A to B is the back-scye depth. A to C is the length to the natural waist. A to D is the length. C1 is at the hip line, and is 5½ inches below C. Square the cross lines from 1, B, C, C1 and D.

C to E is 1½ inch for sizes of 36 bust and over. For less than 36 bust C to E is $\frac{1}{12}$ bust. Draw a straight line from A to E. This establishes F.

F to G is the blade. G to H is ½ inch more than ⅙ bust, 3½ inches for this draft. F to I is a full half of bust. I to 13 is ½ inch. Square up from H and down from G. This establishes T and Q.

On the divisions of two-thirds on the drafting-square we find that the blade size, 10¼ inches, is opposite 15½, which shows that the blade is equal to two-thirds of 31 bust. Now find 15½ on the divisions of fourths, which is 3⅞ inches, and place that amount back from G to J. Square up from J to establish K.

From 1 to L is half of the quantity between G and J. It may be made wider if so desired, as ⅛ bust or ¼ inch less than ⅛ bust.

Draw a straight line from L to I. K to M is $\frac{1}{16}$ bust.

G to 10 is the same as K to M. F to 18 is the same as 1 to M. Connect 18 and M. This establishes 7.

From 7 to 8 is ¼ inch. Shape the scye from 8 as represented, dropping ¼ inch below the bust line.

From 8 to 9 is according to taste or style. On the diagram 8 to 9 is ⅛ bust. Draw a guide-line from 8 to a point midway between E and 2, and shape the back from 9 to 2 as represented, making the width from E to 2 to taste or style. On the diagram E to 2 is 1¼ inch.

Square down from E and 2 to establish 3, 4, 57 and 58.

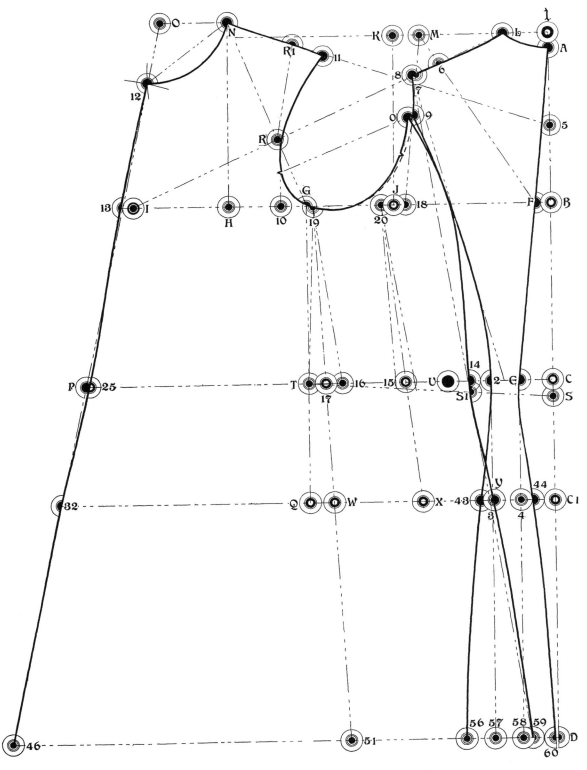

DIAGRAM 5.

From 3 to 43 is ½ inch, and from 4 to 44 is the same.

From 57 to 56 is 1¼ inch, and from 58 to 60 is the same.

Complete the back below E and 2 as represented.

G to N is the front-scye depth less the width of the back A to L. Connect G and N to establish R.

Point 5 is half-way between A and B. Connect 5 and N. Connect M and F to establish 6.

N to R1 is the same as L to 6. F to 6 and G through R to R1 is the over-shoulder.

Shape the shoulder seam from N through R1.

N to 11 is the same as L to 8.

Complete the scye from 11 through G as represented.

Square forward from N. N to O is ⅙ bust. Draw a straight line from O through 13 to establish P, 32 and 46.

N to 12 is ¼ bust for the average form.

In custom cutting point 12 is found as follows only when the garment is to close at the throat, viz.: Take the width of the back from A to L. Place this at N and extend the tape down in a direct line to P. Then holding it at P extend the end up toward O and make a cross sweep at the measure for depth of gorge, 6 inches for this draft. Now apply the measure for the half-size of neck from A to L and N, following the curve of the gorge until the size required, 7¼ inches, intersects the cross-sweep for depth of gorge.

Shape the center-of-front line from 12 passing ⅛ inch forward of 13; ¼ inch back of P, and on through 32 as represented.

T to U is the back-waist. U to E represents the *back-waist surplus*, 3¼ inches for this draft, more than the quantity required by the back-waist measure. As the garment is to be tight fitting through this part this surplus is disposed of as follows:

From T to 16 is one-half of the back-waist surplus. From 2 to 14 is one-fourth of the surplus. From 14 to 15 is half-way from 14 to 16. The remaining one-fourth of the surplus is distributed equally on each side of 15.

Point 17 is half-way between T and 16. G to 19 is ½ inch less than T to 17. Draw a straight line from 19 through 17. This establishes W and 51. From 19 to 20 is ¼ inch less than half-way from 19 to the side of the back. Draw a straight line through 20 and 15. This establishes X.

Connect 9 and the notch at front of scye. From 9 to 0 is ¼ inch.

Reshape the sidebody from 0 as represented.

Draw a line from 8 through 14 as a guide for the run of the sidebody below the waist line, and shape the sidebody from 0 through 14 and Y to 59 as represented. Y is ¼ inch back of the guide line.

The method for obtaining the half-width of the back opposite 5 as above explained applies only to proportionate forms. In custom cutting the measure to determine this width should be taken and applied in the following manner:

F to 18 is the half-back width, and 1 to M is the same. Connect M and 18. This establishes 7. From 7 to 8 is ¼ inch. Now proceed as already explained.

(*Concluded on page 38.*)

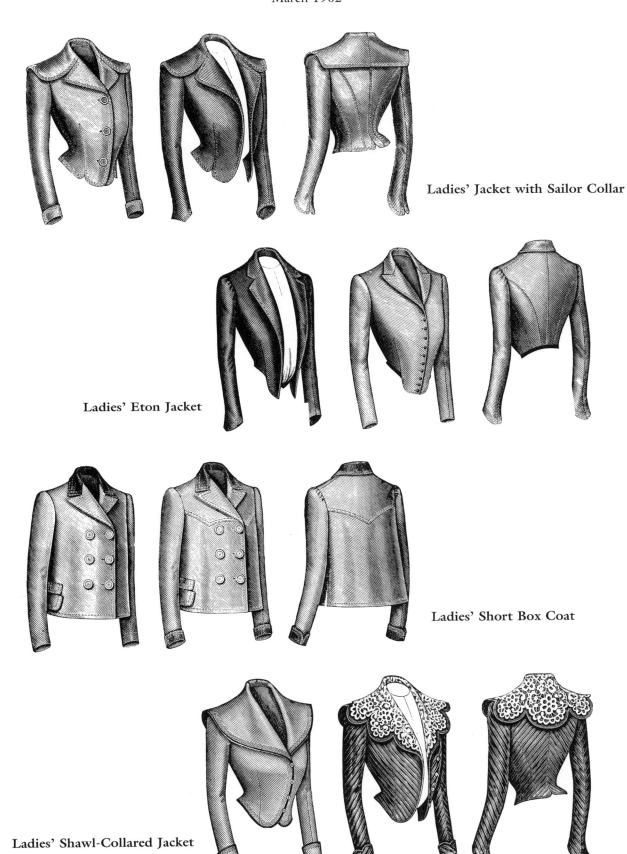

Ladies' Jacket with Sailor Collar

Ladies' Eton Jacket

Ladies' Short Box Coat

Ladies' Shawl-Collared Jacket

Tight=Fitting Jackets.

(*Concluded.*)

DIAGRAM 6.

Points F, J, G, 10 and 13 on the bust line, E, 2, 14, U, 15, 16, 17, T and 25 on the waist line, 32, Q, W, X, 43, 44, Y and C1 on the hip line, and 46, 51, 56, 60 and D on the lower line are obtained as explained for the preceding diagram.

U to V is a full half of the waist. V to 25 represents the *front waist surplus,* 4¼ inches for this draft, which must be taken out by the darts. This surplus is disposed of as follows: First divide the quantity between G and 13 into three equal parts. This establishes 21 and 22. Now divide the quantity between T and 25 into three equal parts. This establishes 23 and 24. Draw straight lines from a point ½ inch back of 21 through 23 to establish 34 and 48, also from 22 through 24 to establish 37 and 49. From 26 to 27 is ½ inch less than one-half of the front-waist surplus, 1⅝ inch for this draft, distributed equally on each side of 23. The remainder of the front-waist surplus, 2⅝ inches, is distributed equally on each side of 24. This establishes 28 and 29.

From 22 to 31 is ½ inch less than ⅓ the distance from 22 to 24 for the average form. *For forms with high or prominent busts point 31 is found by the application of the 15th measure (length to brow of bust), as explained for Diagram 2.* Draw a line from F through 31 to establish 30.

Q to Z is 1 inch less than the front hip.

Z to 32 represents the *front hip surplus* which is taken out by the darts, about one-third distributed equally on each side of 34 and the remainder equally on each side of 37. The front waist length, point 6, is applied in the same manner as explained for Diagram 2. Draw the guide-lines and shape the darts as represented.

Take the width of the back from 43 to 44; place this at Z and measure directly across to the back seam of the sidebody at Y. For this draft this measures 18½ inches, which is 2½ inches less than a full half of the hip size required. This difference is added to the hip size by overlapping the parts below the waist-lines at W and X as follows: Two-thirds of it, 1¾ inch, is distributed equally on each side of W and the balance equally on each side of X.

Draw the guide lines and shape the seams above the hip line as represented.

Below the hip line the seams are continued as follows: Shape the back seam of the underarm piece from the hip line to 55 parallel with the back seam of the sidebody from Y to 59. Shape the side-seam of the forepart below the hip-line to 52 parallel with the back-seam of the underarm piece. Shape the side-seam of the underarm piece below the hip line to 50, nearly parallel with the line W to 51 as represented. Shape the front edge of the sidebody below the hip-line to 53 parallel with the side-seam of the underarm piece.

It must be borne in mind that the length to the natural waist at E is taken *level with the bottom of the waist at the sides, as at T. Quite frequently the waist length*

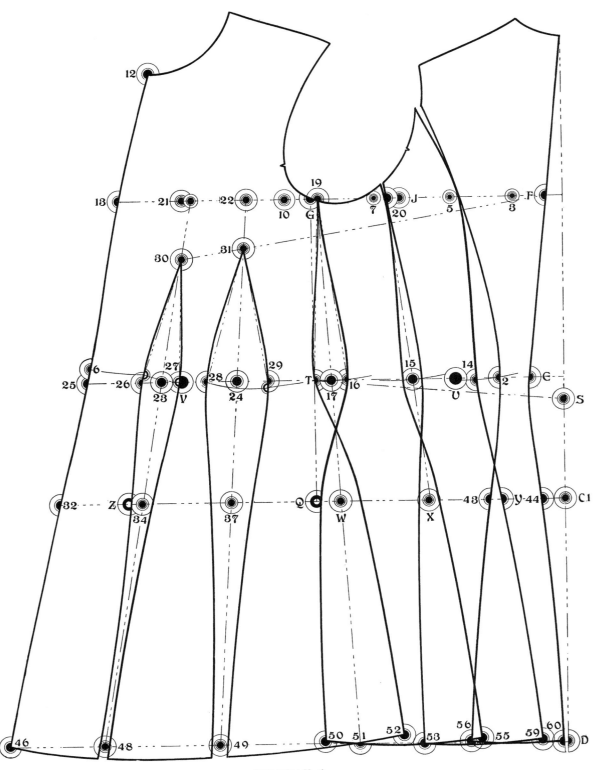

DIAGRAM 6.

is greater at the center of back than it is at the sides. This must be noted when the measures are taken and a memorandum made, as " 15½ length to natural waist, 16¼ length in back."

S represents the waist length at the back. Connect S and T.

All seams through the back-waist must be shaped so that the greatest hollow between the several parts will be on the line S T.

Square up from the middle of the back, sidebody and underarm piece at the waist line to establish 3, 5 and 7 on the bust line.

Cast short sweeps to establish the waist notches, first from 2 forward, pivoting at the side of the back on the bust line, then from 15 pivoting at 20, and from 16 pivoting at 19.

For the run of the bottom sweep across the back from D pivoting at 3. This establishes 56. From the notch just below 14 to 59 is the same as from 2 to 56. Sweep forward from 59 to establish 53, pivoting at 5. From 15 to 55 is the same as from 15 to 53. Pivot at 7 and sweep from 55, to establish 50. From T to 52 is the same as from 16 to 50. Pivot at 12 and cast a short backward sweep from 46 about 6 or 8 inches, and from there shape the bottom to 52 as represented.

The line 12, 13, 25, etc., is at the *center of front*.

As many of the lines below the waist overlap, each part would require piecing to retain the shape as on the draft. To avoid this place a piece of paper underneath the draft, and with a tracing-wheel trace first along the lines which define the sidebody. Then from the piece which is underneath, the pattern can be cut whole. Trace the underarm piece in the same manner. The back and forepart can then be cut out whole. The bust lines and waist notches should be traced on the underarm piece and sidebody.

Early Spring Street Styles
The Delineator
March 1902

For Summer Afternoons
The Delineator
July 1902

TIGHT-FITTING JACKET.

Single Bust Dart.

DIAGRAM 7.

THE measures used for the accompanying diagram are as follows: 5½ half-width of back, 6¾ back-scye depth, 14¾ length to natural waist, 9⅜ blade, 10¾ front-scye depth, 14¾ over-shoulder, 5¾ back-waist, 8½ front hip, 34 bust, 23 waist, 40 hip, 13 brow-of-bust, 19½ front waist length.

All the points on and above the bust-line excepting J, K, S, 2, 3, 4, 8 and 21 are obtained in the same manner as explained for Diagram 5.

All the points on the waist-line, excepting 24 and 26, and all the points on the hip-line excepting 33, 34 and 35, are obtained in the same manner as explained for Diagram 6. The sideback-seam is often extended to the shoulder-seam instead of to the scye, as on the preceding diagrams. From 7 to 8 is ½ inch.

L to J is two-thirds of the quantity between L and 8. Shape the sideback-seam from J to 2 as represented. This establishes 21.

Shape the sidebody from a point ¼ inch forward of J, through 21 and 14 as represented. From 19 to 20 is ¼ inch less than half-way from 19 to 21.

S is half-way between G and 13. From 25 to 24 is to taste or style. On the diagram 25 to 24 is 2¼ inches. From 24 to 26 is the same as from V to 25. Draw a straight line from S down half-way between 24 and 26 to establish 34. In this case the line passes through V, but it may be drawn as much forward of V as required to obtain the desired style effect. N to 30 is the length to brow of bust less the width of the top of the back A to L.

On all tight-fitting fronts the run of the waist-line must be found as follows:

A to L and N in a direct line to 6 is the front waist length. Pivot at 12 and sweep back from 6 to the front of the dart. From there sweep across the dart, pivoting at 30. This line is shown by the light line, running from 6 through 24, and passing below 26 to T. From 34 to 33 is the same as V to 24, except in cases where a large front-hip would require a smaller amount to be taken out by the dart on the hip-line, when it may be made ¼ or ½ inch less. From 33 to 35 is the same as Z to 32. Shape the dart as represented. N to K is the same as L to J.

The fronts as represented close with a fly. The buttonholes may be cut through if preferred. The following method will very greatly aid the student in correctly obtaining the style effects for the fronts.

First establish the front edge below the end of the roll, keeping it as much forward or backward of the center-of-front line as may be deemed necessary after a careful study of the fashion plate. The heavy broken line from 12 to 32 is at the center-of-front. In this instance from the center-of-front line to the front edge is ¾ inch. Draw the lapel crease-line from the end of the roll towards a point 1 inch forward of N. Run a tracing-wheel along this line, and fold the paper which is forward of it, back underneath the forepart. Locate the point of the lapel as at 2, in conformity with its position as shown on the fashion plate, which in this case appears to be about half-way between the bust-line and the top of the shoulder, and half-way between the lapel crease and front of scye.

Establish point 3. This is where the end of the collar joins the lapel. Observe if the top of the lapel from 2 to 3 runs parallel with the bust-line or has a slight or decidedly upward pitch and draw the line accordingly. A glance at the fashion plate will at once determine whether 3 is half-way between the lapel crease-line and 2, or more or less than half-way, and it should be located accordingly.

Having thus established points 1, 2 and 3, trace through on the paper, which is folded underneath, from 1 to 2 and 2 to 3. Unfold the paper and the impressions of the tracer will define the shape of the lapel as from 1 to 4 and 4 to the end of the

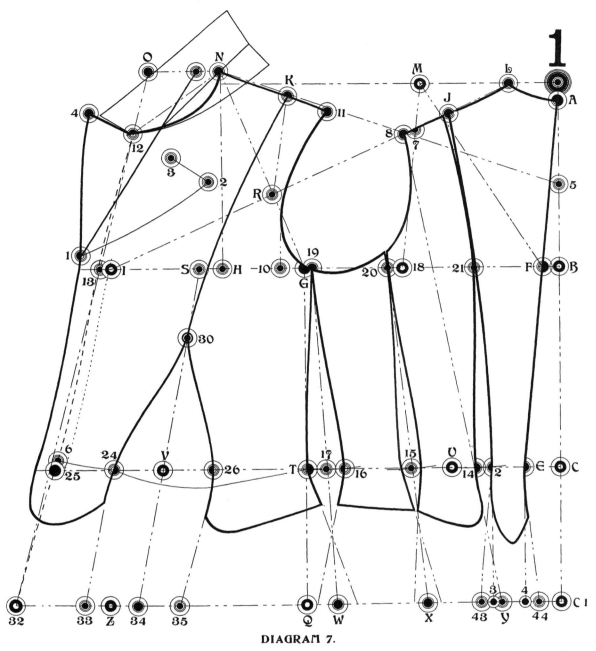

DIAGRAM 7.

gorge, which in this case is a trifle forward of 12. Now shape the gorge from N to the end of the collar. To obtain the run of the bottom, cut out all of the parts leaving a margin of extra length at the bottom of each. Lay the underarm piece with the notch at 16 resting at the notch at T, and the two edges touching each other below the notches. Lay the front edge of the sidebody against the back edge of the underarm piece below the waist notches. Lay the back against the sidebody below the waist notches. With each part in the position described, shape the bottom edge from the center-of-back to the side about 2 inches forward of the line G T Q as the style requires. Take the forepart separately, and bring the edges of the dart to a closed position touching each other below the waist notches. Now shape the bottom of the forepart as required.

For the collar see "Collars," Diagram 42.

BOLERO OR ZOUAVE JACKET.

DIAGRAM 8.

ALL the points on and above the bust line except S and 19 are obtained in the same manner as explained for Diagram 5.

S is half-way between G and 13. Square down from S to establish 23.

C to E is $\frac{1}{12}$ bust.

T to U is the back-waist.

T to 2 is the same as E to U.

Half-way between T and 2 establish 17.

G to 19 is the same as T to 17.

Shape the sideseam as represented.

U to V is half of the full waist.

Square down from 13. This establishes P.

P to 25 is 1 inch.

V to 25 represents the front waist surplus, one-third of which is taken out by the dart from 24 to 26.

These jackets are made in all varieties of lengths and shapes. Two shapes are shown for the front, one extending from the shoulder point at N as represented by the broken line passing through 16, and one from the throat at 12. Shape the fronts to any current style. They are frequently made from 1 to 3 or 4 inches shorter than to the natural waist, and with or without a seam at the center of the back. Sometimes they are cut nearly square across the bottom of the back, as from 2 to 14. Sometimes they are rounded across the bottom, as to 15. They are made with or without collars and revers, which if required, are added the same as for any other style of jacket.

SHORT DART.

DIAGRAM 9.

IT is sometimes desirable that the bust dart extend to the pocket mouth only. This is permissible when the jacket is not to be made tight-fitting through the front waist.

Two shapes are shown on the diagram, the square and the oval. The dart is first drawn in the usual manner. For the square pocket-mouth proceed as follows:

Draw a line parallel with the original waist line in the position desired, and cut the pattern as from 1 to 4.

From 1 to 6 and 8 to 7 are each the same as from 4 to 5. Cut the dart above 4 and 5, and the side-seam from 6 to 7, as represented. When the dart is closed point 1 will be at 6.

For the oval shaped pocket mouth extend the dart below 4 by a graceful curve to the position desired at the sideseam as at 2, and cut the pattern from 2 past 4.

Half-way between 4 and 5 establish 3.

Square up from 3 and 5, and run a tracer along the lines above 3 and 5.

Fold the pattern forward on the line above 3, and then backward on the line above 5. This brings 5 directly over 4.

Press the creases flat; bring that part of the pattern which is below the cut to lie *over* the part above, and mark along the edge of the cut as from 2 to 4. This gives the line from 2 to 5.

When the dart is closed point 2 will be at 9.

Cut out the dart and reshape the sideseam below 9 as represented.

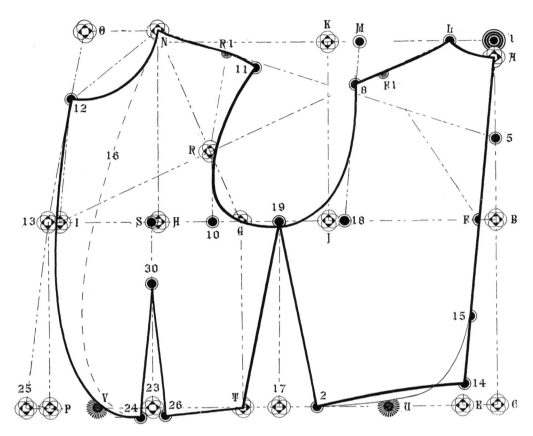

DIAGRAM 8.

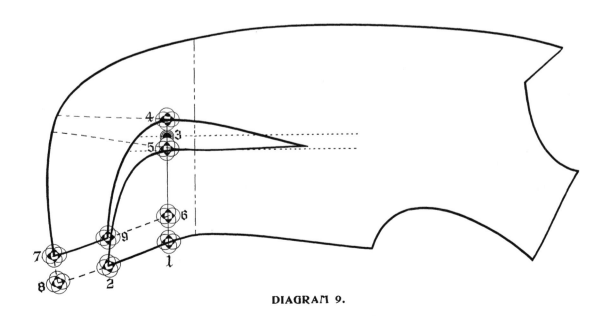

DIAGRAM 9.

DOUBLE=BREASTED SHORT JACKET.

HALF-TIGHT FRONTS.

DIAGRAM 10.

POINTS N, G, I, 12 and 13 are obtained in the same manner as explained for Diagram 5. T, V, Q and Z are obtained in the same manner as explained for Diagram 6.

Square down from 13 to establish P. P to 25 is 1 inch. Draw a straight line from 13 through 25 to establish 32.

The line 12, 13, 25, 32, is at the center of front. Any amount may be added forward of this line as required by the current style. On the diagram 2½ inches is added as from 13 to 1, and the same amount forward of 32.

The revers are formed in the same manner as explained for Diagram 7.

The position of the button-line depends upon the amount which has been added to the fronts forward of the center-of-front line, in connection with the diameter of the button to be used. Should the button be 1 inch or less in diameter, then the button-line should be placed back from the center-of-front line ½ inch less than the amount which has been added in front. Should the button be more than 1 inch in diameter, then the button-line should be placed as much back of the center-of-front line as the front edge has been placed forward, *less one-half of the diameter of the button.*

Locate the buttonholes, and from the eye of each square back by the center-of-front line to establish the position of the buttons on the button-line.

S is half-way from G to 13.

Point 23 is half-way from T to 25.

S to 30 is one-third the distance between S and 23.

The amount to be taken out by the dart depends upon the degree of shapeliness required. It may be ¼, ⅓ or ½ of the front-waist surplus which is represented by the quantity between V and 25. This may be divided equally on each side of 23, or one-third of the amount to be taken out may be taken from 23 to 24 and the remainder from 23 to 26, according to the effect desired.

From 34 to 33 is the same as from 23 to 24.

The quantity to be taken out by the dart on the hip-line should be in the same proportion as that which has been taken out on the waist-line. That is to say, should the width of the dart on the waist-line be made half of the front-waist surplus, then from 33 to 35 will be half of the front hip surplus.

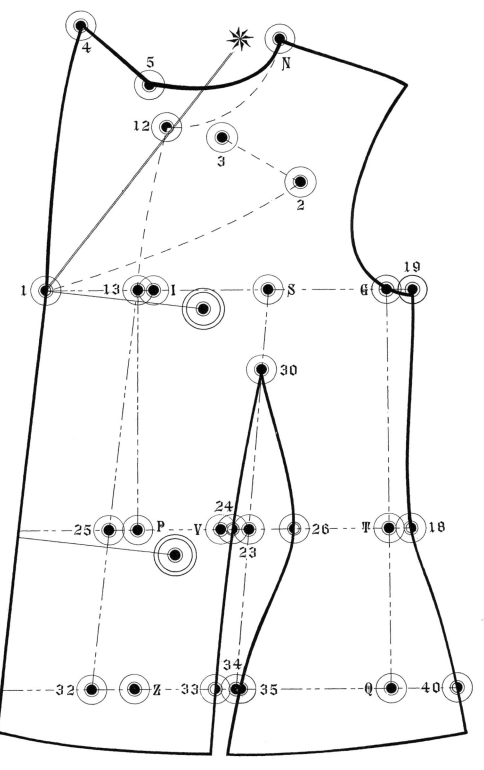

DIAGRAM 10.

DOUBLE=BREASTED SHORT JACKET.

FULL BOX FRONTS.

DIAGRAM 11.

ALL the points are obtained in the same manner as already explained. The style represented is a double-breasted straight front jacket with peaked revers closing at the throat. For a full box front the dart is of course omitted.

THE POSITION OF THE SIDE=SEAM.

FOR all medium and small sizes the position of the side-seam should be as shown on Diagrams 6 and 7. For sizes above 40 bust and when but one side-form is desired, the seam should be placed further back as shown on Diagrams 2 and 10. Care must be taken to so locate this seam as not to produce narrow underarm and sidebody pieces for small or slender forms, nor too wide ones for stout or short forms.

For the largest sizes this seam should be placed as shown on Diagrams 3 and 6, but they should have three side-forms as shown on Diagram 3.

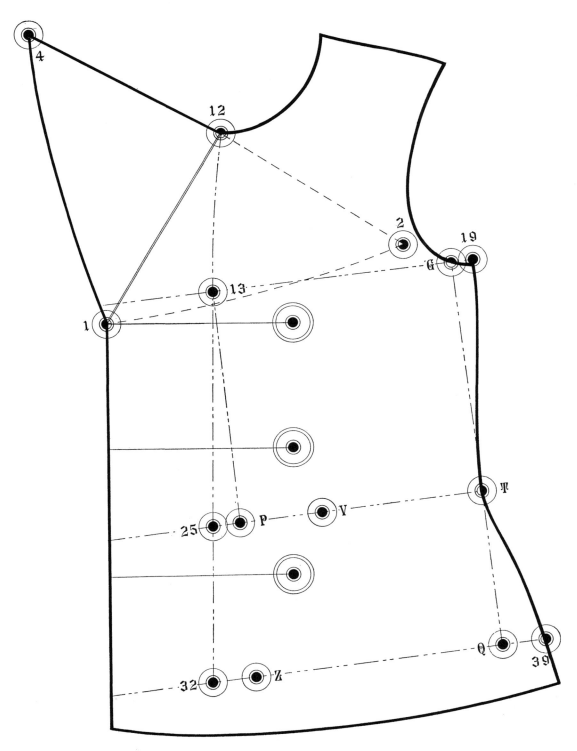

DIAGRAM 11.

JACKETS WITH FULL SKIRTS.

DIAGRAMS 12 AND 13.

ON all of the preceding diagrams the distribution of the size at the hip-line has been made according to the measure as taken on the form. Jackets cut in this manner will, of course, lie plain about the hips.

The style may be either plain or full. But to produce fulness or drapery below the waist proceed as follows:

The broken lines below the waist represent the outlines of a back and sidebody drafted as heretofore instructed. A is at the natural waist, B is 1 inch below A, and C is at the hip line, 5½ inches below A.

For a full-skirted coat add 1 inch from E to G, also from D to F, and draw straight lines from the edge of the pattern at line B through F and G.

The sweeping point for the run of the bottom is at A.

Additions may be made in like manner for fulness to the underarm piece and to the side-seam of the forepart as will be determined by the current style. For garments more than 38 inches in length, not more than ½ inch should be added on either side, as this will give ample fulness.

WHOLE BACKS.

DIAGRAM 14.

FIRST shape the back as for a seam from 2 to 3, and from 6 to 4, in the usual manner.

Extend the center line from 2 to 5.

From 4 to 7 is the same as 3 to 5.

Sweep forward from 5, pivoting at 2 to establish 7.

Finish as represented.

*　　　*　　　*

TO CHANGE A BACK WHICH HAS BEEN CUT WITH A CENTER-SEAM TO A WHOLE BACK, proceed as follows:

Draw on the paper a straight line as the line 1 to 5.

Lay the back on this line to touch at 1 and 2, and mark around it above the waist.

Pivot the back at 2 and swing the bottom forward until 3 is at 5. Mark around it from 8 to 7 and 7 to 5.

The solid lines represent the changed pattern.

When cutting the material let 1 and 5 be flush with the fold of the goods.

In making up, the material must be stretched opposite 6 the amount lost between 6 and 8, and well shrunk at 2.

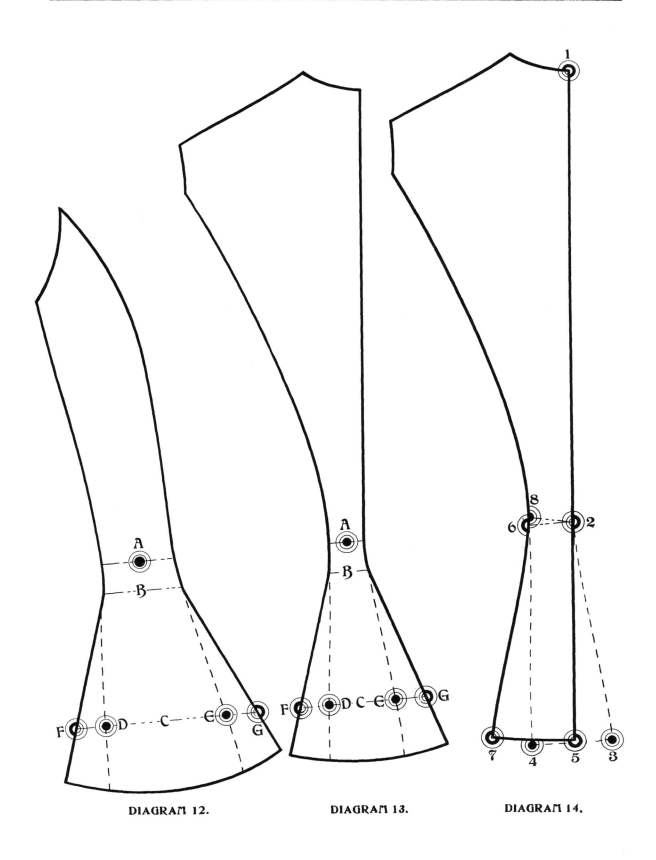

DIAGRAM 12.   DIAGRAM 13.   DIAGRAM 14.

LOOSE=FITTING SACK JACKET.

DIAGRAM 15.

THE measures used for the accompanying diagram are as follows : $5\frac{5}{8}$ half-back width, 7 back-scye depth, $15\frac{3}{4}$ length to natural waist, 24 length, $9\frac{1}{2}$ blade, $11\frac{1}{4}$ front-scye depth, $15\frac{1}{4}$ over-shoulder, $8\frac{1}{2}$ front hip, 35 bust, 23 waist, 40 hip.

TO DRAFT.

Draw a straight line as from the heavy circled disk and square across from the same point. From the heavy circled disk to A is $\frac{1}{24}$ bust.

A to B is the back-scye depth. A to C is the length to natural waist. A to D is the length. C to C1 is $5\frac{1}{2}$ inches. Square across from B, C, C1 and D.

C to E is $\frac{3}{4}$ inch. Draw a straight line from A to E. This establishes F. Shape the back below E through C1 as represented.

From the heavy circled disk to M is the half-back width, and from F to 18 is the same. Connect M and 18.

F to G is the blade. G to 10 is $\frac{1}{4}$ inch less than $\frac{1}{16}$ bust. G to H is $\frac{1}{2}$ inch more than $\frac{1}{6}$ bust. F to I is half of full bust. I to 13 is $\frac{1}{2}$ inch. Square up from 10 and H and down from G and I. This establishes T, Q and P.

P to 25 is 1 inch. Draw a straight line from 13 through 25. This establishes W.

From the heavy circled disk to L is $\frac{1}{8}$ bust. Connect L and I. This establishes 7. From 7 to 8 is $\frac{1}{4}$ inch. J is $1\frac{1}{2}$ inch above the bust line, and $\frac{1}{2}$ inch forward of the line M to 18. Shape the back-scye from 8 to J.

E to 2 is 1 inch less than $\frac{1}{2}$ waist. Shape the side-seam from J through 2 as represented. The width of the back at J, 2 and S may be increased or diminished according to taste or style.

G to N is the front-scye depth, less the width of the top of the back A to L. Point 5 is half-way from A to B. Connect 5 and N. Connect F and M to establish 6. N to 9 is the same as L to 6.

F to 6 and G through R to 9 is the over-shoulder. N to 11 is the same as L to 8. J to K is $\frac{1}{4}$ inch. Finish the scye from 11 through G to K, dropping $\frac{1}{4}$ inch below the bust line. As the form is not corpulent, no further attention need be given to the waist measure.

Q to Z is the front hip. C1 to X, and Z to Y is 1 inch more than half of the full hip. Shape the side-seam from K through Y as represented.

Square forward from N. N to O is $\frac{1}{6}$ bust. Connect O and 13. N to 12 is $\frac{1}{4}$ bust.

The line 12, 13, 25, W is the center-front line. The quantity to be added forward of this line, and the shape of the lapels are determined by the prevailing style. This has been fully explained in the explanation of Diagram 7. On the diagram from 13 to 1, and W to U, are each 3 inches.

Pivot at a point midway between the heavy circled disk and M, and sweep forward from midway between D and S. This establishes S. From 18 to T at the bottom is the same as from 18 to S. Pivot at 12 and sweep forward to U, also sweep a short distance back from W. Shape the bottom from T to U as represented.

The side-seam of the forepart may be made less shapely between 18 and Y, but should not be drawn forward of 2 on the waist-line.

If it is desired that the coat shall be more shapely at the waist, the back-waist measure should be taken and applied as from T to V on the waist-line. V to E would then represent the back-waist surplus. One-third of this may then be taken out by the underarm cut as represented by the lightly dotted lines falling from the

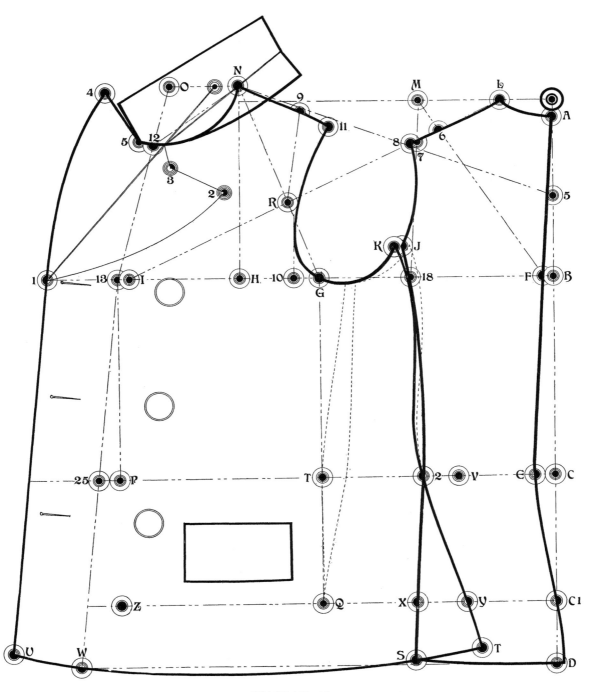

DIAGRAM 15.

bottom of the scye and terminating at Q. This cut must be ½ inch wide at the top so that the necessary seam allowance may be left on the material when cut. The side-seam must then be drawn ½ inch back of the position shown on the diagram on the bust line, and terminating at the waist line as represented by the lightly dotted line just back of 18.

For the Collar, see "Collars," Diagram 42.

TIGHT-FITTING JACKET.

Vest Effect.

DIAGRAM 16.

THE measures used for the accompanying diagram are as follows: 5½ half-back width, 6¾ back-scye depth, 14¾ length to natural waist, 9⅜ blade, 10¾ front-scye depth, 14¾ over-shoulder, 5¾ back-waist, 8½ front hip, 34 bust, 23 waist, 40 hip, 12½ to brow of bust, 19 front-waist length.

The jacket represented by this diagram may be made from materials of a contrasting color, as a gray homespun for the body part, and a white ladies' cloth for the vest effect, revers, collar, cuffs and pocket flaps. The front closes with a fly.

All the dark-centered points on the back and shoulder sections are correspondingly lettered and numbered, and are obtained in the same manner as explained for Diagram 5.

All the dark-centered points through the waist and hip sections, except 44, are obtained in the same manner as explained for Diagram 6.

The side-seam of the back is drawn straight towards 3. In such cases from 4 to 44 is 1 inch.

The points which locate the position of the darts—points 23 and 24—are not always arbitrarily established as explained for Diagram 6. Frequently it is required that they be placed further forward to secure the desired style effect. In such cases the width of the part between 25 and 26 may be first established as on the diagram, which is made 1½ inch. Then from 26 to 27 will be ¼ inch less than one-half of the front-waist surplus. In this case the width of the tongue between 27 and 28 is 1½ inch. From 28 to 29 is the remainder of the front-waist surplus. Point 23 is now established half-way between 26 and 27, and 24 half-way between 28 and 29.

From 34 to 33 is ¼ inch less than from 23 to 26.

From 37 to 36 is ¼ inch less than from 24 to 28.

From 36 to 35 is ½ inch more than from 27 to 28. This establishes the width of the dart on the hip-line between 33 and 35.

From 36 to 38 is the same as Z to 32 less the width of the first dart from 33 to 35.

To secure the desired style effect the front dart is extended through 21 to the gorge.

Establish the front edge and shape the revers and the bottom edge in the same manner as explained for Diagram 7.

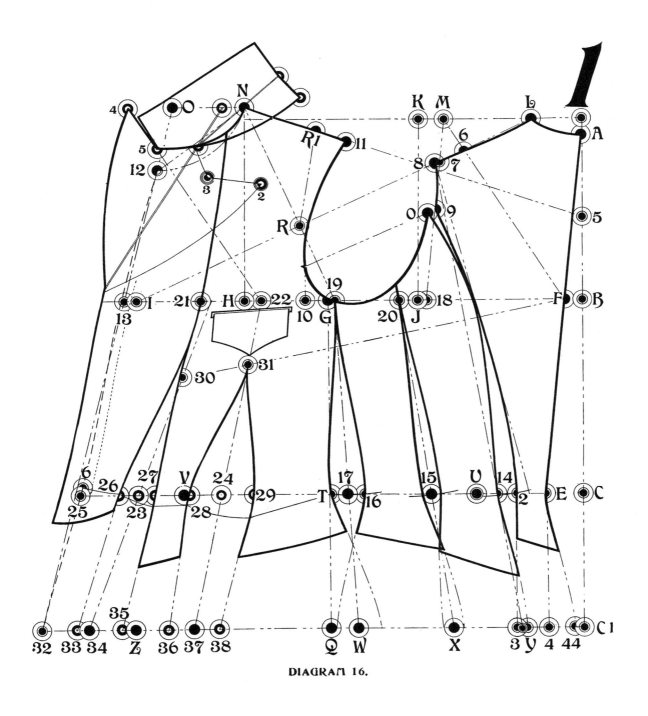

DIAGRAM 16.

DOUBLE=BREASTED FROCK COAT.

THE BACK AND BODY.

DIAGRAM 17.

THE measures used for the accompanying diagram are as follows : 6¼ half-back width, 7¼ back-scye depth, 15¾ natural waist length, 17¾ fashionable waist, 35½ length, 10½ blade, 11¾ front-scye depth, 15⅞ over-shoulder, 6¾ back-waist, 9½ front hip, 13½ to brow of bust, 20½ front-waist length, 38 bust, 27 waist, 44 hip.

The back is drafted in the same manner as explained for Diagram 5, except that from E to 2 is 1½ inch. It may be made to style or taste. Side and center-back plaits are added below the fashionable waist length at 17 and 18.

The body, back of the center-of-front line, is drafted in the same manner as explained for Diagrams 5 and 6 with the following exceptions :

The underarm-seam is drawn ½ inch back of the position it occupies on Diagram 6, and the width of the part forward of the first dart on the waist line is made 2 inches. About ½ inch less than half of the front-waist surplus is then taken out by the first dart. The tongue between the darts is from 1 inch to 1¼ inch wide, and the remainder of the front-waist surplus is the width of the second dart.

N to 16 is the front-waist length, less the width of the top of the back. Sweep back from 16, pivoting at 12 to establish 15.

Establish 14, 11 and 10 as explained for Diagram 2.

The front hip, Q to Z, in connection with the full hip, must be utilized to determine the run of the lines below the waist-line as explained for Diagram 6.

The position of the waist-seam is determined by the prevailing style. On the diagram from 16 to F is 2 inches, 9 to K is 1 inch, 8 to L is the same as 9 to K, and 2 to 17 is 2 inches.

From the waist notch just below 5 to O is the same as from 2 to 17. Draw straight lines from O to L and K to F.

Cut out the pattern, all except the gorge N to 12, leaving about 1 inch of paper across the bottom of the forepart below the broken line F K, and on the underarm piece and sidebody below the broken line L O.

Lay the several parts in closing position below the waist notches as shown on the small diagram below, and shape the bottom edge from O through K to F. This establishes G, H, I, J, M and N.

THE LAPEL.

Place a piece of paper underneath the pattern of the forepart, mark along the edge from the top of the first dart to G, then to F, and up past 12.

Make a cross-mark as at A.

Cut out the lapel as thus far defined, notching both forepart and lapel at A. Place the lapel in closing position with the forepart above the notches at A, and draw the crease-line from opposite the top buttonhole towards a point 1 inch forward of the shoulder-point N.

Fold the upper part of the lapel on the lapel-crease line underneath the forepart. Draw on the forepart the shape of the lapel to style, and mark the same through by a tracing wheel on to the paper, which is folded underneath, as from the end of the roll at 1 to 2 and thence to 3.

On unfolding the paper the upper part of the lapel will be defined by the points 4 and 5. Now shape the gorge from N to 5.

Cut out the pattern and proceed to draft the skirt as explained for the next succeeding diagram.

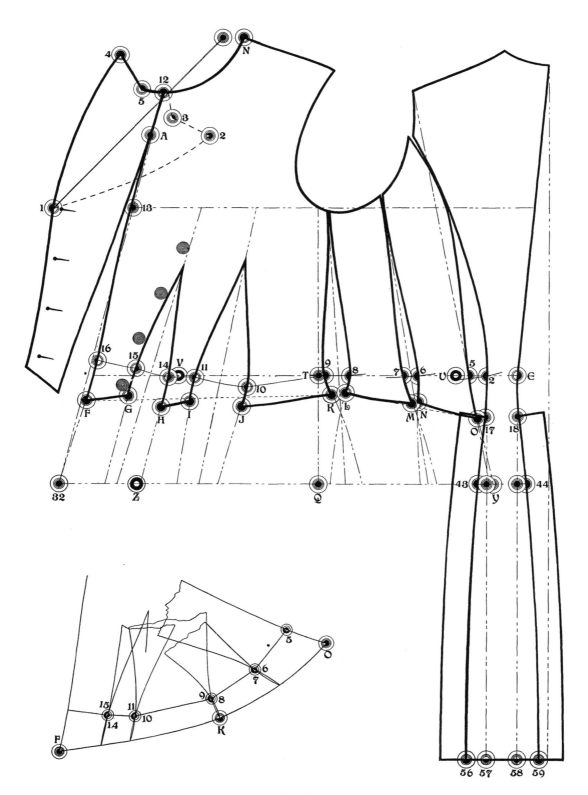

DIAGRAM 17.

Double=Breasted Frock Coat.

(*Concluded.*)

DIAGRAM 18.

Points 5, 6, 7, 8, 9, 10, 11, 12, 13, 14, 15 and 16 are the same as on the preceding diagram.

TO DRAFT THE SKIRT.

Square the lines A B and A C.

A to B is 5½ inches. Square out from B.

A to C is ⅓ waist, and B to D is the same. Draw a line from D up through C.

C to E is ½ waist. Pivot at E and sweep from D towards F, and from C towards 5.

Lay the pattern of the forepart with the line from 15 to 16 directly over the line A C, and 16 as much back of A as it is from the straight line from 12 to 32 on the preceding diagram, viz., ¼ inch. Place a weight on the pattern and extend the straight line from 12 through 13 and A down towards Q. Mark along the front edge of the pattern from 16 to H and across to J.

Lay the tongue, which is between the darts, to touch at J, and with the notch at 11 on the line A C. Mark along the bottom from J to K.

Lay the remaining part of the forepart to touch at K, with 9 on the sweep line from C to 5. Mark along the bottom from K to L, also up along the underarm seam above L.

Lay the underarm piece as represented to touch at L and with 7 on the sweep line C5. Mark along the bottom to M and a short distance up on each side.

Lay the sidebody to touch at M and with 5 on the sweep line C5. Mark along the bottom, M to N, and a short distance above M and N.

B, following the hip line to F, is one-half of the full hip less the width of the back from 43 to 44 (Diagram 17).

Draw a straight line from N through F.

N to O is ¼ inch more than the length of the back-skirt 17 to 56 (Diagram 17.) Shape the plait-edge from N to O passing ¼ inch back of F, and add 1¼ inch for the plait.

Sweep from O through P, pivoting at E, and straighten the bottom from P towards S.

Lay the lapel in closing position with the forepart and add the width and shape of the bottom of the lapel from H to R. Shape the front from R to S parallel with the line H Q, or to style.

A skirt drafted in this manner will have a considerable amount of drapery below the hip line. When less drapery is desired proceed as follows:

Establish points 1 and 2 midway between the overlappings of the sidebodies and forepart above L and M, and draw straight lines from 1 through L to establish T, also from 2 through M to establish U.

Cut the pattern from L and M to the hip line. Spread the cut open 1 inch at L and ½ inch at M, overlapping the paper at T and U. The effect can be readily seen by referring to Diagram 20.

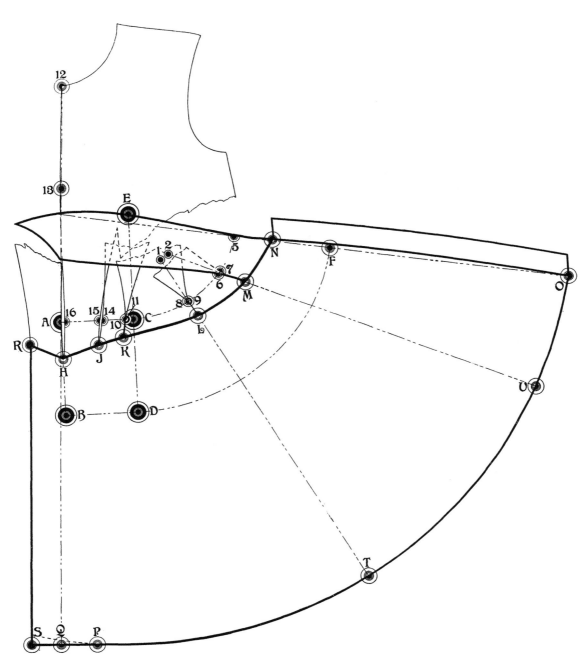

DIAGRAM 18.

CUTAWAY FROCK-COAT.

DIAGRAM 19.

THE back and body are drafted to the measures in the same manner as explained for Diagrams 5 and 6, except that the lapel-seam is in this case omitted and the front edge is drawn to the desired style.

The skirt is drafted in the same manner as explained for Diagram 18, except that the line which is drawn from 12 through 13 where it intersects with the line from 15 to 16 (on Diagram 17) is placed directly over point A, with the line from 15 to 16 over the line A C. In all other respects proceed in the same manner to establish all of the points, and shape the front to taste or style.

To produce the skirt with less drapery establish points 1 and 2 midway between the overlaps of the sidebodies and forepart as shown by the broken lines above L and M. Draw a straight line from 1 through L to establish T, and from 2 through M to establish U. Proceed as explained for the succeeding diagram.

DIAGRAM 20.

Take the pattern of the skirt which has been drafted as explained for the preceding diagram, and mark on it with a tracing wheel the lines L T and M U.

Fold the front underneath on the line L T, and fold the back under on the line M U.

Open out the folds and cut the pattern down on the lines L T and M U from L and M to the hip line. The ends of the cuts are represented by points A and D.

Place a weight on the pattern near the front and spread the cut at L open 1 inch to B.

Press the overlap (T to C) at the bottom flat and secure by a pin.

Spread the cut at M open ½ inch to E.

Press the overlap (U to F) at the bottom flat and secure by a pin.

Reshape the bottom from H to O and shape the darts as shown by the solid lines.

On the material the darts should terminate 1 inch above the hip line.

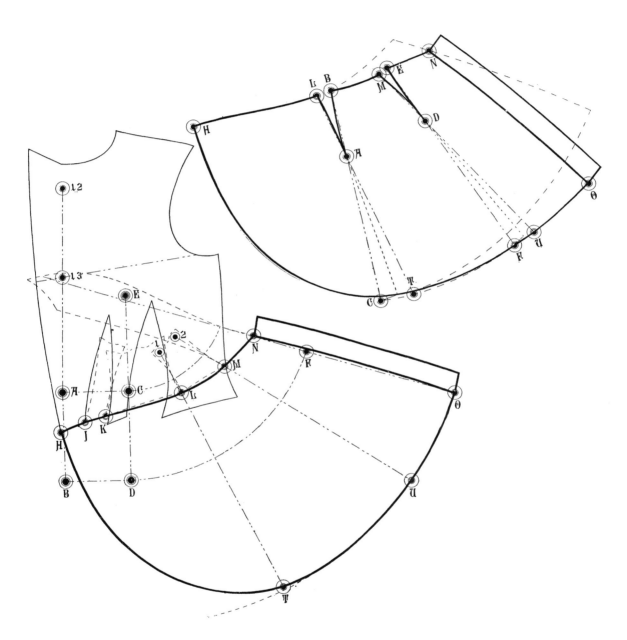

DIAGRAMS 19 AND 20.

ETON JACKET.

WITH SEAMLESS COLLAR.

DIAGRAM 21.

THE accompanying diagram is for the jacket illustrated in the sketch given above. The closing of this jacket is made with olives. The facings are made of material in suitable contrast with that of the body of the jacket. The strappings are of satin. It may also be made collarless.

The measures used for the accompanying diagram are as follows : 5¾ half-back width, 7 back-scye depth, 15½ length to natural waist, 10 blade, 11¼ front-scye depth, 15½ over-shoulder, 6¼ back-waist, 13½ to brow of bust, 20 front waist length, 36 bust, 25 waist.

TO DRAFT.

Square the lines 1K and 1C.

From 1 to A is $\frac{1}{24}$ bust.

A to B is the back-scye depth.

A to C is the length to the natural waist.

Square the cross lines from B and C.

C to E is $\frac{1}{12}$ bust, for sizes of 36 bust and under. For sizes more than 36 bust C to E is 1½ inch. Connect A and C. This establishes F.

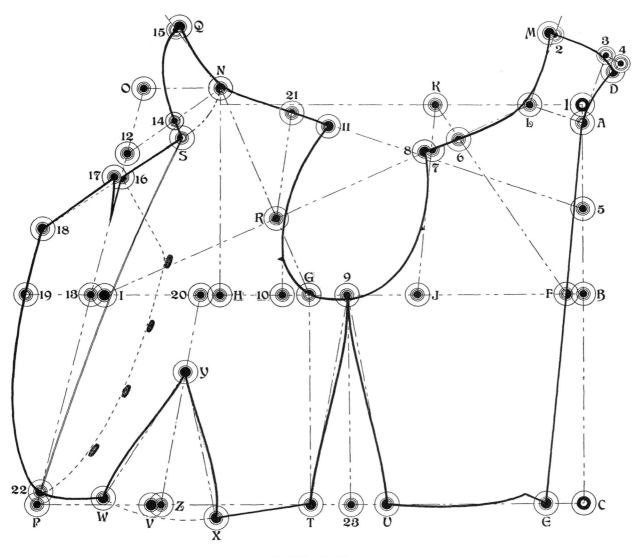

DiAGRAM 21.

F to J is the half-back width, and 1 to K is the same. Connect J and K.

F to G is the blade. G to H is ½ inch more than ⅙ bust. F to I is half of full bust.

I to 13 is ½ inch.

Square down from G to establish T.

From 1 to L is ¼ inch less than ⅛ bust. Connect L and I. This establishes 7.

From 7 to 8 is ¼ inch.

Shape the back-scye from 8 to G, dropping ¼ inch below the bust line at 9.

Connect A and L, and by this line square up from A and L. A to 3 and L to 2 are each 3 inches. From 3 to 4 is ¾ inch. From 2 to M is ¼ inch. Shape the shoulder seam from M, passing ¼ inch forward of L and on to 8, and the back from A towards 4 as represented. From 4 to D is ¾ inch. Shape the top of the back from D to M.

G to 10 is ¼ inch less than $\frac{1}{16}$ bust. Square up from 10 and H. G to N is the front-scye depth less the width of the back from A to L. Connect F and K to establish 6. Connect G and N to establish R. Half-way between A and B establish 5. Connect 5 and N. N to 21 is the same as L to 6.

F to 6 and G through R to 21 is the over-shoulder. In this instance the over-shoulder measure brings 21 on the line N5. A longer or shorter measure would locate this point either above or below the line, as the case may be. The line N 5 gives the run of the front shoulder about right for the average form.

N to 11 is the same as L to 8.

The front scye notch is $\frac{1}{12}$ bust above 10.

Complete the scye from 11 to G as represented.

Square forward from N. N to O is ⅙ bust. Draw a straight line from O through 13. This establishes P. N to 12 is ¼ bust. Point 14 is half-way between N and 12. Square up from N by the line N 12. N to 15 is the same as L to 2. From 15 to Q is ¼ inch. Shape the front shoulder from Q passing ¼ inch above N, and the collar from Q through 14. From 14 to S is ¾ inch. From 12 to 16 is 1 inch. Draw a straight line from S through 16 towards 18. From 13 to 19 is 2½ inches. A to L and N in a direct line to 22 is the front waist length. Shape the front from 22 through 19 and establish 18 as represented. From 16 to 17 is ⅜ inch. The V is 1¾ inch long.

E to U is the back-waist. Point 23 is half-way between T and U.

G to 9 is the same as T to 23.

Draw the guide lines and shape the underarm seam from 9 to T, and 9 to U as represented.

E to U and T to V is half of full waist. T to Z is ¾ inch more than half-way from T to P. Point 20 is half-way from G to 13. Connect 20 and Z.

A to L and N to Y is the length to brow of bust.

Pivot at 12 and sweep back from 22 towards W.

Z to W is half of the quantity between V and P.

Pivot at Y and sweep back from W towards X.

W to X is the same as P to V.

Finish as represented.

When the two fronts are closed in half double-breasted form the edge of the top side is represented by the broken line from 16 to 22. The fronts are closed on this line by four olives and loops placed as illustrated. A pleasing effect is also given by turning the fronts back on the light double-line from S to 22.

For a collarless jacket shape the top of the back from A to L in the usual manner, and the gorge by the broken line from N through S.

Ladies' Capes
Edward B. Grossman & Co.
1900 catalog

Ladies' Skirts
Edward B. Grossman & Co.
1900 catalog

SINGLE=BREASTED BOX COAT.

DIAGRAM 22.

THE measures used for the accompanying diagram are as follows : 6 half-back width, 7 back-scye depth, 15¼ natural waist length, 28 length, 10¼ blade, 11½ front-scye depth, 15¾ over-shoulder, 6½ back-waist, 9¼ front hip, 37 bust, 26 waist, 43 hip.

All the drafting lines and points except the following are the same, and are obtained in the same manner, as explained for Diagram 15.

The fronts close with a fly.

From 13 to 1 and from W to U are each 1½ inch.

The side-seam of the forepart is shaped nearly straight between K and Y.

When the draft has been completed in all other respects as explained for Diagram 15, the center-back-seam is then drawn from A to 15, or to 16 as represented by the solid lines.

From 15 to 16 is 1 inch.

From 10 to 14 is ¼ bust.

Square down from 14 for the front of pocket opening.

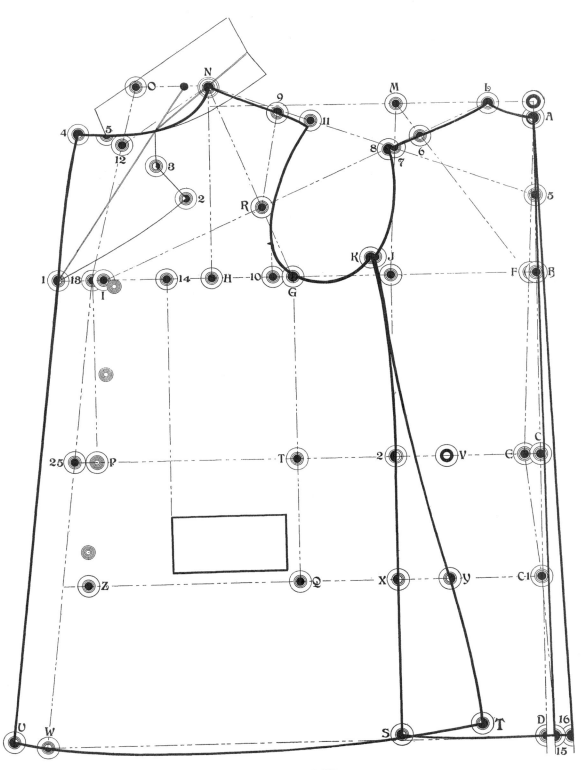

DIAGRAM 22.

PLAIN SLEEVE.

DIAGRAM 23.

THE sleeve is drafted from the following measures: 17½ scye, 9½ underarm-scye, 8 length to elbow, 17 length, 8½ cuff, 11½ elbow.

The scye is obtained by measuring from the outer shoulder point of the forepart at 11, following the line of the scye through 9 to 8 of the back. (See Diagram 5.)

To obtain the second measure, first locate the front-scye notch $\frac{1}{12}$ bust above 10, and the back-scye notch ¼ of the full scye above the bust line, which is just above 9. Now measure from the front to the back notch following the edge of the scye which is represented by the broken line.

TO DRAFT.

Fold a piece of paper, thus forming a crease-line. Open out the fold and lay the paper with the hollow of the crease on the under side. The heavy line from star to star represents the crease-line. A to C is ¼ of the full scye. C to D is the length to the elbow. C to E is the length. C to B is the same as from the bust line to the sleeve notch at front of scye on the forepart. B to the star at the bottom is 24 inches always. From the same star to 1 is 1 inch.

Draw a straight line from 1 through B. This locates A just forward of the crease-line.

Square back from A and C by the line A1, and extend the line from C forward across the paper.

A to F is ¼ of the full scye, and F to G is the same. Square up from F.

F to I is $\frac{1}{12}$ of the full scye. G to H is $\frac{1}{16}$ of the full scye.

Lay the pattern of the forepart over the draft with the bust-line directly over the line which is squared across from C, and the notch at front of scye touching the crease-line as at B. Mark along the edge of the scye from 3 to B and up past 2, as represented by the broken line.

Lay the underarm-piece at 3, keeping the bust line over the line squared back from C, and mark along the top edge to 4.

Lay the sidebody at 4, keeping the bust line over the line squared back from C, and mark along the top edge.

From a point ⅝ inch above 4, as at 5, shape the under-sleeve to B, passing ¼ inch above 3.

Apply the measure for the underarm-scye from B, following the solid line through 5 to N.

Finish the underarm-scye from N to 5 as represented.

From 2 to 6 is ⅝ inch. Shape the top-sleeve-head from H through I and 6 to B as represented. Sweep from E towards M, pivoting at G. E to M is one-half the full size at the cuff. D to O is 1½ inch. It may be made more or less than 1½ inch according to the curvature desired at the elbow. Square back from O by the line E O. O to J is one-half of the size at elbow. J to K and J to L are each ½ inch. Draw guide lines from N to L and M, and from H to K and M, and shape the back-seam as represented. Shape the bottom from E to M as represented.

* * *

It is often required that the backarm-seam be transferred from the position shown on the diagram at H and N to the sidebody. As now drafted it would join the back just above 9 on Diagram 5. When this is the case make a cross-mark and notch the sidebody at the point desired as at 7.

To transfer the seam from H and N to 7 see Diagram 24.

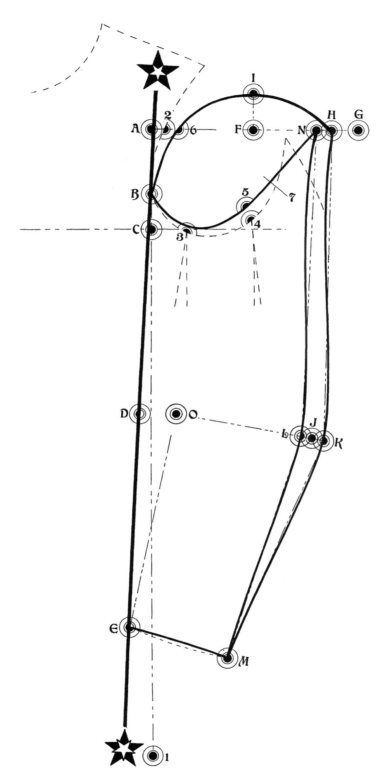

DIAGRAM 23.

Plain Sleeve.

(*Concluded.*)

DIAGRAM 24.

All the points except 6 and 9 are obtained in the same manner as explained for the preceding diagram.

From 7 to 6 is 1 inch.

Sweep from 6 towards 9 pivoting at J.

Transfer the back-seam (which is shown in broken lines below N to L) to 6 and L as shown by the solid line.

The amount which has thus been taken from the under-sleeve as it was originally drafted, is added to the top-sleeve, as from the broken line falling from H on the sweep line to 9, and the round of the top-sleeve is continued from H to 9.

Should it be desired to transfer the seam under the hand, the seam may be drawn below L from ½ to 1 inch forward of the position it now occupies on the diagram at the bottom, and the width of the top-sleeve at the bottom must be increased the same amount.

Having thus far completed the draft with the backarm-seam established either at N and H, or at 6 and 9, as may be required, fold the paper on the original crease-line and cut through both thicknesses of the paper from H, or 9, as the case may be, following the round of the top sleeve to B, also from H or 9 through K to the bottom and across the bottom to the crease line.

Again open out the pattern and cut singly from N or 6, as the case may be, through L to the bottom, and from N or 6 to B. Make a notch at B.

DIAGRAM 25.

The pattern will now appear as outlined by points 6, B, 9, K, M, E, and O to 6, the back-seam having been cut on the lines from 6 through L, and from 9 through K, on Diagram 24.

To place the forearm-seam somewhat back from the center of the front proceed as follows:

Fold the pattern on a line as from 2 to 3, which is ½ inch from the first crease-line, and establish X half-way from K to L.

X to Y is one-half of the full size at the elbow.

Draw guide-lines from 2 to Y and from Y to 3, and shape the forearm-seam as represented.

Cut through both thicknesses of the paper from 2 through Y to 3, and notch both parts at Y.

The small angular piece on the top-sleeve from E to 3 should be cut off from E to 4.

The top-sleeve must be stretched up and down at Y.

This sleeve will have about 2 inches of fulness which must be shrunk into the scye.

From 9 to M will be about ½ inch more than 6 to O. This ½ inch is shrunk to the undersleeve at the elbow.

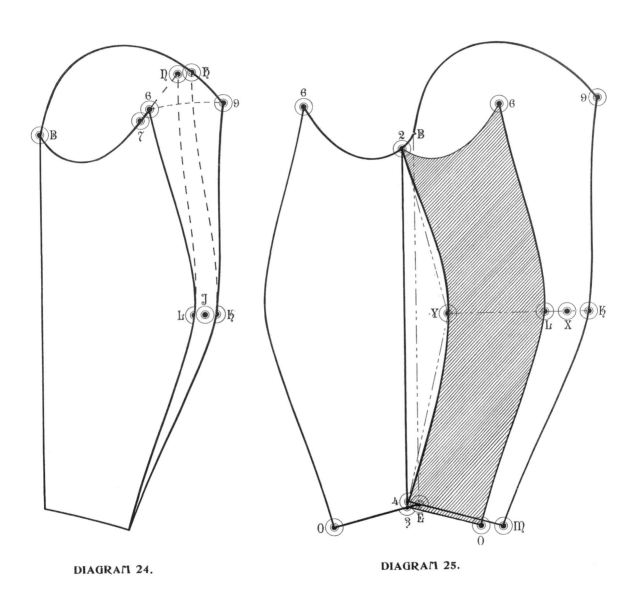

DIAGRAM 24.   DIAGRAM 25.

SLEEVE WITH ENLARGED TOP.

A PLAIN sleeve may be enlarged to any current style as shown on this and the following diagrams for enlarged sleeves.

DIAGRAM 26.

On this diagram is shown a top-sleeve; the width of the sleeve-head remaining the same as that of the plain sleeve, but with one degree of height added to the round.

The plain sleeve, which has been drafted as explained for the preceding diagrams, is shown by the solid lines below 9 and the notch at front of scye, and by the oval shaped broken line from the notch to 9.

Before cutting out the pattern as heretofore explained, draw a straight line across from the notch to 9. Point 3 is half-way between the notch and 9.

Pivot at 3 and cast a sweep from the notch to 9. Shape the round of the sleeve-head as represented by the solid line.

Additional height may be given by squaring up from 3 and raising the sweeping point as much above 3 as may be required to obtain the desired effect. The under-sleeve remains unchanged.

DIAGRAM 27.

On this diagram is shown a sleeve having both added height and width at the sleeve-head over that which obtains for a plain sleeve.

The amount to be added to the height or to the width, also whether all of the added width shall be placed at the backarm-seam, or a part to the forearm-seam, depends upon the effect to be produced. On this diagram the added width has been equally divided on the front and back seams.

TO DRAFT.

Take a plain sleeve which has been drafted as explained for Diagrams 23, 24 and 25. Lay the pattern of the top-sleeve over another piece of paper and mark along the edge of the pattern across the bottom and up on both sides to the elbow, or above the elbow to the point at which it is desired that the enlargement shall begin. The broken lines represent the plain sleeve-head.

Draw a short line up from about the center of the round of the plain sleeve-head, as at A. Establish B and C each 1 inch from A, or as much more as may be required to obtain the effect desired. Pivot at the elbow notch and swing the pattern forward until A touches B. This establishes D.

Mark from the notch to D and down to the notch at the elbow.

Lay the pattern of the plain sleeve in the first position, then pivoting at the back-seam opposite the elbow notch, swing the pattern until A touches C. This establishes E.

Shape the back-seam below E to the elbow as represented by the solid line.

Draw a straight line from the scye notch to E.

Point 3 is half-way between the scye notch and E.

Pivot at 3; cast a sweep from the scye notch to E, and shape the round of the sleeve-head as represented by the solid line.

Any amount of extra height may be given to the sleeve-head as the current style may require by raising the sweeping point an inch, more or less as required. In such case the sweep should be flattened on each side, above E as well as above the scye notch. The under-sleeve remains unchanged.

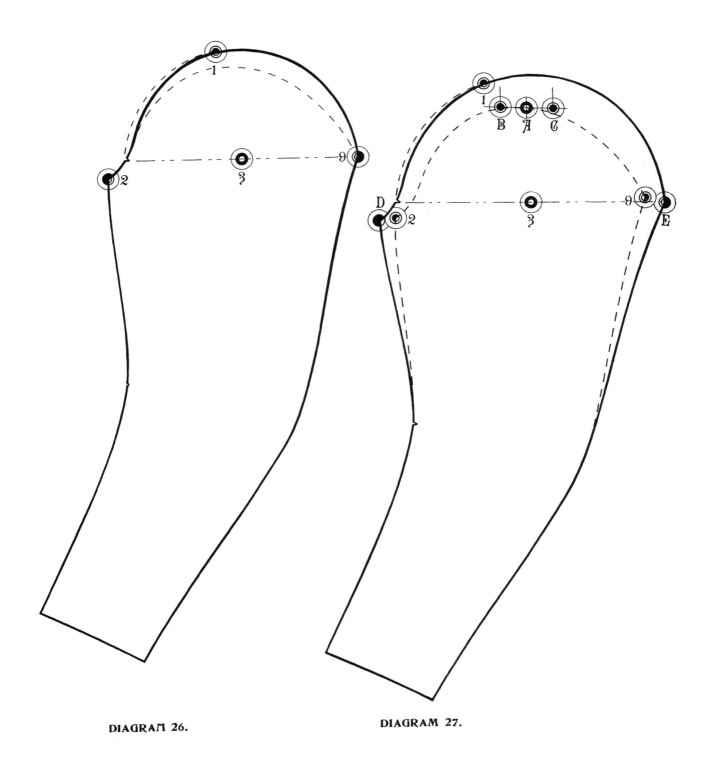

DIAGRAM 26.   DIAGRAM 27.

Sleeve with Enlarged Top.

(*Concluded.*)

DIAGRAM 28.

On this diagram is shown an enlarged top-sleeve, having added height and width greater than that on the preceding diagram. Most of the added width is placed on the back-arm-seam.

TO DRAFT.

Lay a pattern of a plain top-sleeve over another piece of paper. Mark along the edge of the pattern across the bottom and up on each side to as far above the elbow as it is desired that the enlargement shall begin, as to 4 and 5. Also make a cross-mark to indicate the height of the round of the plain sleeve-head.

The plain top-sleeve is defined by the solid lines below 4 and 5, and by the broken lines from 2 to 4, and from 5 to 9 and 2.

From 2 sweep forward, pivoting at 4, and from 9 sweep backward, pivoting at 5.

From 2 to D is $\frac{1}{16}$ of the full scye.

From 9 to E is $\frac{1}{4}$ of the full scye.

Pivot the pattern at 4 and swing the upper part forward until 2 is at D.

Mark along the edge from 4 to D and up just past the scye notch.

Shape from E to 5 as shown by the solid line.

Connect E and the scye notch.

Half-way between E and the scye notch establish 3.

Square up from 3.

The sweeping point may be made at 3, 6 or 7, according to the amount of increased height which it is desired shall be given to the sleeve-head over that of the plain sleeve, which must be determined by the current style. On the diagram from 3 to 6 is 1 inch, and from 3 to 7 is 2 inches.

Cast a sweep from the scye notch to E, pivoting at 3, 6 or 7, and shape the round as represented by the solid line.

The same principle obtains for the enlargement of all two-piece sleeves.

From 9 to E may be made as much as the full scye according to the effect desired.

The under sleeve remains unchanged.

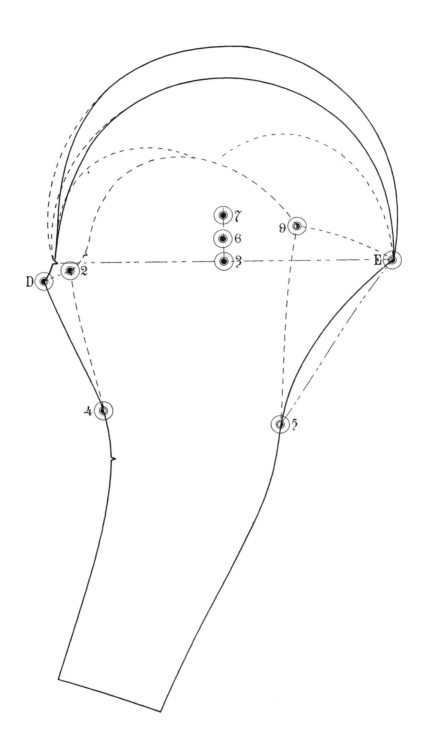

DIAGRAM 28.

DART SLEEVES.

DIAGRAM 29.

THE fulness in the top sleeve is sometimes taken out by darts. The sleeve is first drafted with more or less increased width and height at the sleeve-head to give room over the point of the shoulder and to secure the style-effect required.

A plain sleeve is first drafted. This plain sleeve has been enlarged on this diagram the same degree as the one shown on Diagram 27.

Before cutting out the enlarged pattern, square up from 3 to establish A.

Measure the top-scye of the coat (Diagram 5) from the notch at front of scye to 11, then from 8 to 9 and 0 to the back-scye notch below 0. This we will suppose to be 9 inches.

Now measure the enlarged sleeve-head from the front-scye notch following the round to E. This we will call 16 inches. The difference between the two (which will now be 7 inches) is the amount to be taken out by the darts. On this diagram it is taken out by five darts in the following manner:

Distribute one-fifth, or 1⅜ inch, equally on each side of A as from A to 1, and A to 2.

Connect 1 and E, also 2 and the scye notch.

Divide the quantities between 1 and E, also between 2 and the notch, each into three equal parts. This establishes B, C, D and F.

Draw straight lines from 3 through B, C, D and F, to establish G, H, J and K, and make the remaining darts the same width as from 1 to 2.

Pivot at 3 and cast a sweep at the height of the top of the plain sleeve-head as shown by the broken line, and shape each dart to this line as represented.

The top curve of the sleeve-head should be shaped between the darts as shown by the solid lines.

The under sleeve remains unchanged.

For four darts, proceed as follows, having in mind that the size of the top-scye of the coat is 9 inches, and the amount to be taken out by the darts is 7 inches as before.

From the scye notch to the first dart is ⅕ of the top-scye of the coat. Each dart is ¼ of the full amount to be taken out. Each of the parts between the darts will be the same as from the scye-notch to the first dart.

Draw lines from the center of each dart to 3, and complete the sleeve as heretofore explained.

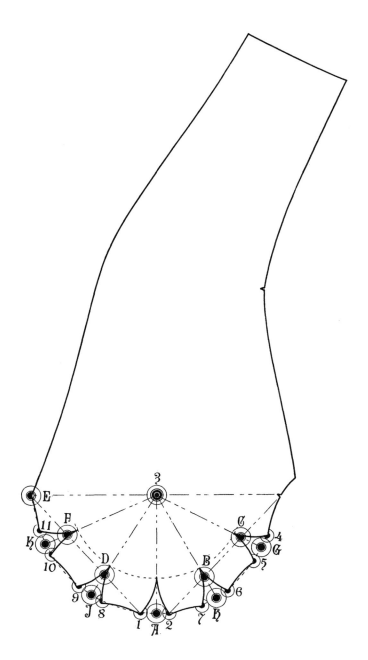

DIAGRAM 29.

ENLARGED SLEEVE.

(MEDIUM FULL LEG-O'-MUTTON.)

DIAGRAM 30.

THIS sleeve is cut in one piece. The enlargement is partly made at the front, but the greater part is added at the back. It is drafted as follows:

Place on another piece of paper the top part and the under part of a plain sleeve pattern, to touch each other at M and O, and about 1 inch apart at K as represented.

Mark along the edge of the underpart from 6 to 2, Y, 3 and O, and along that of the top part from M to 3 and Y.

Sweep from 2 towards C, pivoting at Y.

From 2 to C is 2 inches.

Hold the pattern at Y; swing 2 over to C, and mark along the edge of the paper from Y to C.

Mark up a short distance above B.

Draw a straight line from C to 6.

F is half-way between C and 6.

Square up from F.

F to G is 2 inches. (It may be made more or less than 2 inches according to the effect desired.)

Sweep from 6 to C, pivoting at G, and shape the round from B to D as represented.

Cut out the pattern on the solid lines, making notches at Y, Y and B.

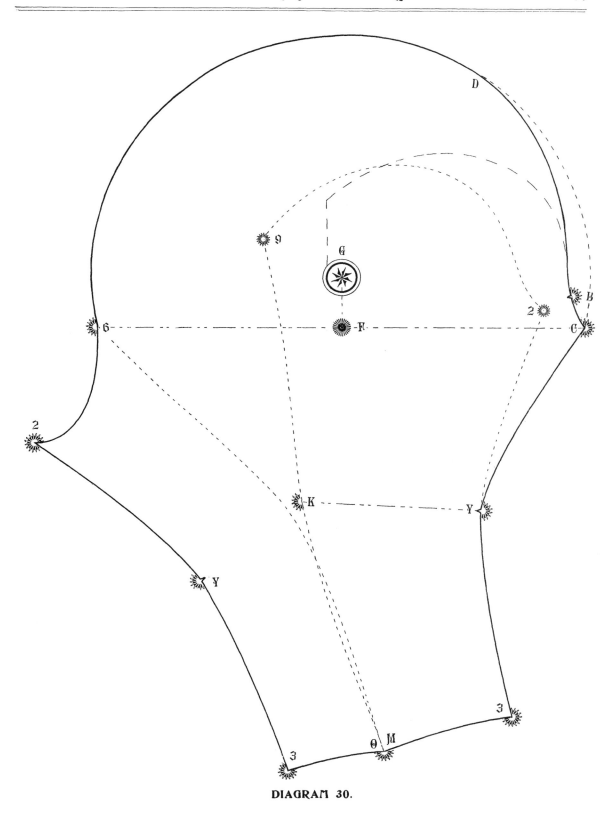

DIAGRAM 30.

ENLARGED SLEEVE.

(Full Leg-o'-Mutton.)

DIAGRAM 31.

TAKE a pattern of a plain sleeve and lay the top part and the under part on another piece of paper so that they will touch each other at the elbow and open about 1 inch at the bottom as from M to O.

Mark along the edges below the notches at YY.

Pivoting at Y sweep from 2 towards C, and from 2 towards E, according to the amount of extra width required, 3 inches for a medium, and 4 inches for an extra full sleeve.

Holding the top sleeve at Y, swing point 2 over until it reaches C and mark from C to Y.   Also holding the under part at Y swing point 2 until it reaches E, and mark from E to Y.

Draw a straight line from C to E.

F is half-way between C and E.

Square up from F.

F to H is 4 inches.

Sweep from E to C, pivoting at H.

If less height is required sweep from G, which may be placed 1, 2 or 3 inches above F.

Reduce the sweep from E to 1, or E to 5, to give a semblance of an underarm sleeve-head, also from B to 7 or 8 as illustrated.

The sleeve is closed at the bottom with buttons.   A button-stand is therefore added to the under side 1 inch in width.

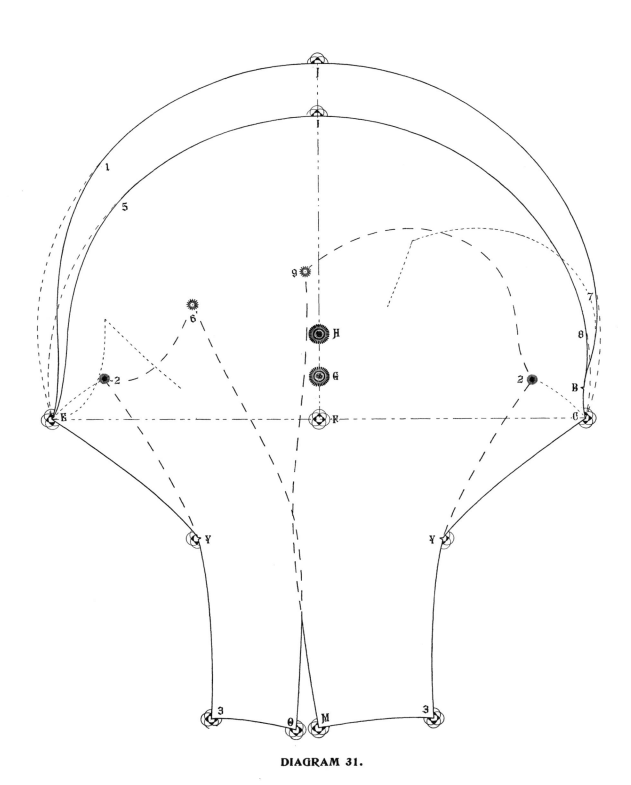

DIAGRAM 31.

BELL OR WING SLEEVE.

DIAGRAM 32.

A PLAIN sleeve drafted as explained for Diagram 24, having the back-seam at H and N at the top is represented on this diagram. Points B, E, H and N are therefore obtained in the same manner as for Diagram 24.

B to 1 and E to 2 are each $\frac{1}{12}$ scye.

When cutting out the pattern, leave about 1 inch of paper on the top part from H to the elbow as represented on the diagram.

Cut through on the line from 1 to 2.

DIAGRAM 33.

Paste the parts together as shown on this diagram, to touch at H and at the elbow, and make a mark near the middle of the round of the top part as at 5.

DIAGRAM 34.

Draw a straight line as C D.

Lay the pattern (Diagram 33) with the round of the sleeve-head touching the line C D, in the position shown by the shaded part on the diagram.

Make a cross-mark at 5.

Letting the round of the sleeve-head follow along the line C D, gradually raise point 1 until it is about 1 inch above the line C D, as at F. Place a weight on the pattern and make a cross-mark at the notch, which gives E.

Mark along the edge of the pattern from the notch to 1. This establishes F.

Mark along the edge of the pattern from 1 towards 2. This gives the line F G.

F to G is the underarm length for the wing sleeve.

Lay the pattern (Diagram 33) again in the position shown by the shaded part, and gradually raise point 3, letting the top of the sleeve-head follow along the straight line C D, until 3 is as much above D as F is above C. This establishes H.

Mark along the upper edge of the sleeve-head to H.

K is half-way between C and D.

Square up and down from K.

K to L is ½ inch.

Shape the top of the sleeve from the notch through L as represented.

Extend the line F G to establish M, and pivoting at M, sweep from G to N.

Cut the paper from F through L to H, and make a notch at E.

Fold the paper on the line L N, observing that H is directly underneath F, and cut through both thicknesses from F to G and from G to N.

F to G seams on to H to P.

It should be observed that the top of the sleeve is made plain, having the same amount of fulness as is given to a plain sleeve. These sleeves are sometimes made with more fulness at the top. Additional fulness may be obtained as follows:

Establish two points as represented by the two small stars on the line C D, placing them as far apart as required for the extra fulness at the sleeve-head. Lay point 5 at the star at the left and swing the pattern from there to establish F, as previously explained, and then lay the same point at the star at the right, and swing to establish H.

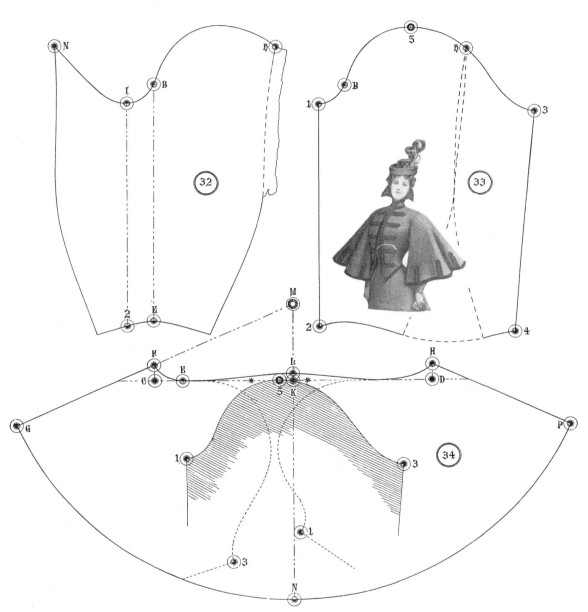

DIAGRAMS 32, 33 AND 34.

COLLARS.

DIAGRAM 35.—This military collar will hug the neck close at the upper edge. Square the lines 1 to 2 and 1 to 3.

From 1 to 3 is 1 inch. From 3 to 2 is ¼ inch less than the size of the neck-gorge. Shape the seam-edge from 2 to 3, as represented.

Square up from 3 by the seam-edge towards 4, and make 3 to 4 and 2 to 5 the fashionable width.

DIAGRAM 36.—This collar will not cling as close to the neck on the upper edge as the one shown on the preceding diagram. It is drafted on squared lines from 1 to 2 and 1 to 4.

From 1 to 2 is ¼ inch less than the size of the neck-gorge.

1 to 4, and 2 to 5 are each made the fashionable width.

DIAGRAM 37.—This collar will stand away from the neck on the upper edge, because of the curve given to the seam-edge from 2 to 3.

Square the lines 1 to 2 and 1 to 4.

From 1 to 3 is 1 inch, and 3 to 2 is ¼ inch less than the size of the neck-gorge. From 3 to 4, and 2 to 5 is the fashionable width. From 4 to 6 is ¼ of the width of the collar. Shape as represented.

DIAGRAM 38.—This collar will stand away from the side of the neck on the upper edge still more than the one shown on the preceding diagram. It is drafted in the same manner as for the preceding diagram, excepting that from 1 to 3 is 2 inches, and 4 to 6 is ¼ of the width of the collar.

DIAGRAM 39.—The upper edge of the collar defined by points 2, 3, 5 and 6, will have a decided flare from the side of the neck. It is drafted in the same manner as for the preceding diagram, excepting that from 1 to 3 is 3 inches. Additional flare may be given to the upper edge of the collar by making it in two pieces each side. In such a case proceed as follows :

From 3 to 7, and 7 to 8 are each the same as the width of the top of the back of the coat. Pivot at 3 and cast a short sweep just above the top edge of the collar, also (using the same length of sweep) pivot at 8 and cast a cross-sweep as represented to establish 9. Connect 7 and 9.

From 10 to 11 is the same as 4 to 6 distributed equally on each side of the line from 7 to 9.

The front portion of this collar is defined by points 2, 7, 11, 5 and 2, and the other portion by 3, 6, 10, 7 and 3.

DIAGRAM 40.—This collar is made in two parts, the stand being drafted in the same manner as the one shown on Diagram 35, and is defined by points 1, 2, 4 and 5.

The leaf is defined by points 4, 6, 7, 8 and 9, and is produced as follows :

Reverse the position of the stand as shown by the shaded part and mark around the edge lightly. Shape the seam-edge from 4 passing through 6, (which is ½ inch inside of the edge of the shaded part), towards 5. From 4 through 6 to 7 is the same as the top of the stand from 4 to 5.

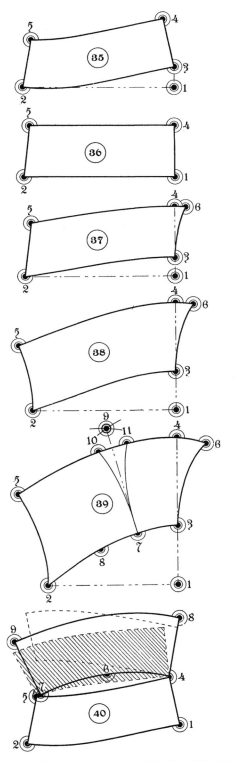

DIAGRAMS 35, 36, 37, 38, 39 AND 40.

Lay the pattern of the stand in the position shown by the upper broken lines, and mark along the back seam to get the run of the back seam of the leaf from 4 to 8.

Make from 4 to 8, and 7 to 9 the fashionable width, and shape the bottom of the leaf from 8 to 9 as represented by the solid line.

The principle involved in drafting collars with a stand only, and also those having both a stand and leaf, is that the more convex the sew-on edge is made, and the more concave the upper or outer edge, the less will be the spring, and the closer will the upper or outer edge cling to the neck. On the other hand, the more concave the sew-on edge is made, and the more convex the outer or upper edge, the greater will be the spring of the collar and the ease with which it will fall around the neck.

DIAGRAM 41.—This collar is designed for garments which close at the throat. It is usually worn with the leaf turned down over the stand, but can be worn standing when desired. It is drafted in the following manner:

Lay the pattern of the forepart over another piece of paper and mark the shape of the neck-gorge from 1 to 2. Shape the end of the collar above 1 to style.

Remove the pattern and shape the crease-line from 1 through 2 towards 3, and the seam-edge from 1 towards 4, passing about 1 inch below 2.

From 1 to 4 is ¼ inch less than the size of the neck-gorge, and from 3 to 4 is 1¼ inch.

From 3 to 5 is the fashionable width of the leaf. The line 3 to 4 is square with the crease-line, and that from 3 to 5 is sprung out about ¼ inch from a straight line if one were drawn from 4 through 3.

DIAGRAM 42.—This is also a stand-and-fall collar. It is suitable for all coats which close high over the bust, also for those with medium length of roll, and for soft rolls. It is drafted as follows:

Lay the pattern of the forepart over another piece of paper. Mark the shape of the neck-gorge from 4 to 8, and shape the end of the collar to style.

Draw the crease-line from 3 through 4 towards 5. From the crease-line to 6 is 1¼ inch. Shape the seam-edge from 6 to 8 as represented, making from 8 to 6 ¼ inch less than the size of the neck-gorge.

Square by the crease-line from 6 to establish 5. From 5 to 7 is the fashionable width. For a leaf of medium width, the back seam from 5 to 7 should be sprung out about ¼ inch from a straight line drawn from 6 through 5.

DIAGRAM 43.—This collar is designed for coats with long rolls. It is a stand-or-fall collar, and is drafted in the same manner as explained for the preceding diagram, except that the crease-edge is drawn from 3 midway between 2 and 4.

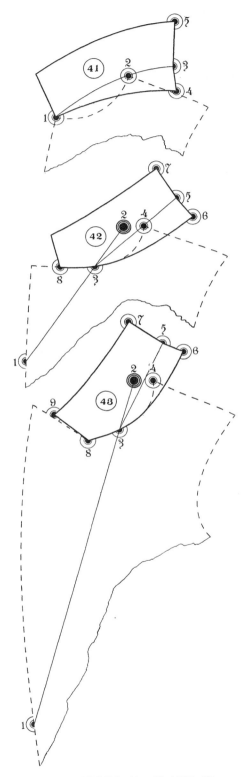

DIAGRAMS 41, 42 AND 43.

PLAIN AND RIPPLE COLLARETTES.

THE plain collarette is produced as follows :

Lay the pattern of the front and back of the garment touching each other at the shoulder-seam.

Mark along the edge from 1 to the center of the front at 3, and down the center of the front towards 4.

Mark across the top of the back from 1 to 5, and down towards 6.

From 5 to 6 is the width.

Extend the line from 4 up through 3, and the one from 6 through 5 until the two lines intersect as at the heavy circled disk.

Sweep from 6 to 4, pivoting at the heavy circled disk, or shape the outer edge of the collar to any desired style.

This defines that part of a plain collarette which lies over the shoulders. It may be surmounted by any desired style of collar, joined by a seam from 3 to 5.

To produce the ripple effect proceed as follows :

From 3 to 7, 7 to 8, 8 to 1, and 1 to 5 are each one-fourth of the neck-gorge from 3 to 5. Draw the lines from the heavy circled disk through 7, 8 and 1 to establish 9, 10 and 11.

Cut through on the lines below 7, 8 and 1. Lay the pieces over another piece of paper, keeping the parts together at 7, 8 and 1, and about 2 inches apart at 9, 10 and 11, as shown on Diagram 45.

The collarette is often cut without a seam at the gorge, in which case proceed as follows :

Cut the pattern through on the lines 7 to 9, 8 to 10 and 1 to 11, as drafted on Diagram 44. Lay the pieces on another piece of paper and mark all around them as from 3 to 7, 9, and 4 to 3, as shown on Section 1 below the diagrams.

Draw straight lines across each from 3 to 7, 7 to 8, 8 to 1, and 1 to 5.

Square up from 7, 8, 1 and 5, and make the height of the stand as desired. This gives 12, 13, 14, 15, 16, 17 and 18. From each of these points add to the spring of the upper edge ½ inch, or as much as required according to the amount of flare desired. On Section 4 the center-back-seam is sprung out from 18 one-fourth of the height from 5 to 18.

To produce the ripples at the part which lies over the shoulder, add 1 inch, or more if required, from 9 of Sections 1 and 2, from 10 of Sections 2 and 3, from 11 of Section 3, and from 11 and 6 of Section 4.

Shape each part as represented by the solid lines.

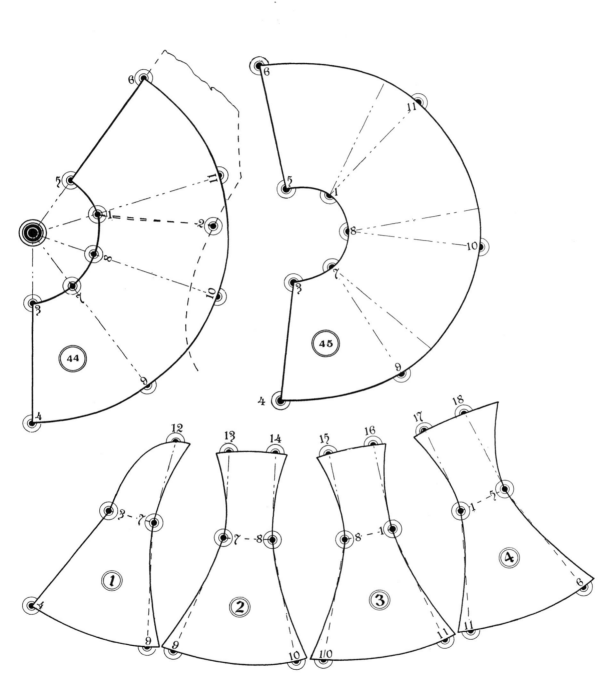

DIAGRAMS 44 AND 45.

BROAD COLLARS.

DIAGRAM 46.

LAY the back and forepart over another piece of paper to touch each other at A and B as represented by the broken lines. From 1 to 3 is the depth required. From 3 to 6 is the width.

Shape the neck of the collar from 1 through A to 4.

Point 4 is at the style depth in front.

Shape the outer edge according to style as from 4 to 5 and 6.

When it is desired that the collar shall lie less close over the shoulders proceed as follows :

Draw a straight line from 1 to 7. (Point 7 is the same as 12 on Diagram 5.)

Half-way between 1 and 7 establish 8.

Pivot at 8 and sweep from A towards 9.

A to 9 is the same as A to 1.

Draw a straight line from 9 parallel with the line 1 to 7.

From 9 to 10 is the depth desired.

From 10 to 11 is the width.

Shape the neck of the collar from 9 through A to the depth required in front as to 4, and the outer edge to style, or as from 4 to 5 and 11.

DIAGRAM 47.

This sailor collar differs from the one shown on the preceding diagram only in that a stand has been added. The stand is added on to the top of the back between 1, 2, 3 and A and is represented by the shaded part. It is also added on to the forepart between 3, 5 and B, which is also shaded.

From 1 to 2 is ¾ inch.

A to 3 is ¾ inch.

B to 3 is ¾ inch.

Lay the forepart and back over another piece of paper, to touch each other at 3, and ½ inch apart from A to B. The positions of the back and forepart are shown in broken lines.

Shape the neck of the collar from 2 through 3 and 5 to the length required in front as to 6.

From 2 to 4 is the depth.

From 4 to 8 is the width.

Shape the outer edge as represented from 6 to 7 and 8, or to taste or style.

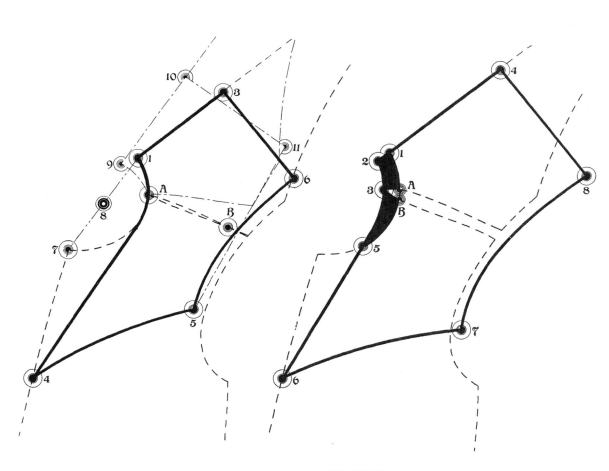

DIAGRAM 46.   DIAGRAM 47.

THREE=QUARTER OR MILITARY CAPE.

———

DIAGRAM 48.

DRAW a straight line as A B.

Take the back and forepart of the waist or coat over which the cape is to be worn, and lay the back to touch the straight line at 1, which is ⅜ inch below A, and 1½ inch forward of the line at the waist, as at E. The position of the back is shown in broken lines. Mark from A past the top point of the back as shown by the solid line.

Lay the front shoulder ½ inch from the back as shown by the broken lines, and mark along the gorge to the center of the front at C, and down the center-of-front line towards D.

Connect A and C.

F is half-way between A and C.

Square in from F.

F to G is 2 inches.

A to B is the length.

Sweep for the bottom from ½ inch above B toward D, pivoting at G, and re-shape the bottom from B and D to the sweep, as shown by the solid line.

Any amount may be added forward of the center-of-front line C D, or taken from it, according to the style effect to be produced, the same as for any other style of garment. The gorge is usually surmounted by a stand-and-flare, or a stand-and-fall collar.

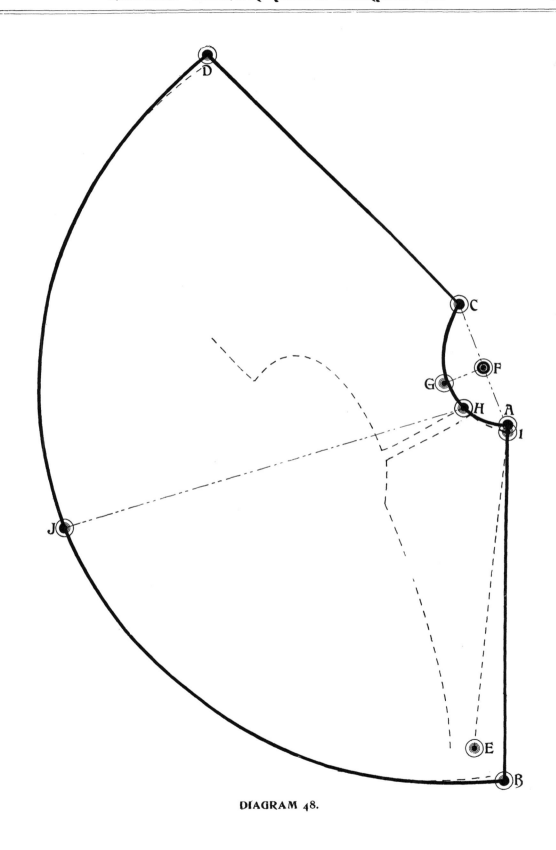

DIAGRAM 48.

HALF=CIRCLE CAPE.

DIAGRAM 49.

POINTS A, B, C, D, H and J are the same as on the preceding diagram, point J being half-way between B and D.

Connect H and J, and establish K ¼ of the bust from H.

Fold the pattern of the ¾ cape on the line H J, and cut the pattern from H to K.

Open out the pattern, keeping the hollow of the crease from K to J underneath.

Place a weight on the back part of the pattern, raise the crease at J, and pivoting at K fold J back towards O, until the center-of-front line C D is square with the line A B. This will spread the cut at H open to N.

Press the fold in the paper flat, and mark from H to K and K to N, along the neck-gorge to L and down the center-of-front line to M.

Extend the line from A to B up towards Q, and square back from L by the line A B to establish Q.

Q to the circled disk is 1 inch.

Pivot at the circled disk and cast a sweep from B to M as shown by the solid line.

Shape the shoulder-seam as represented.

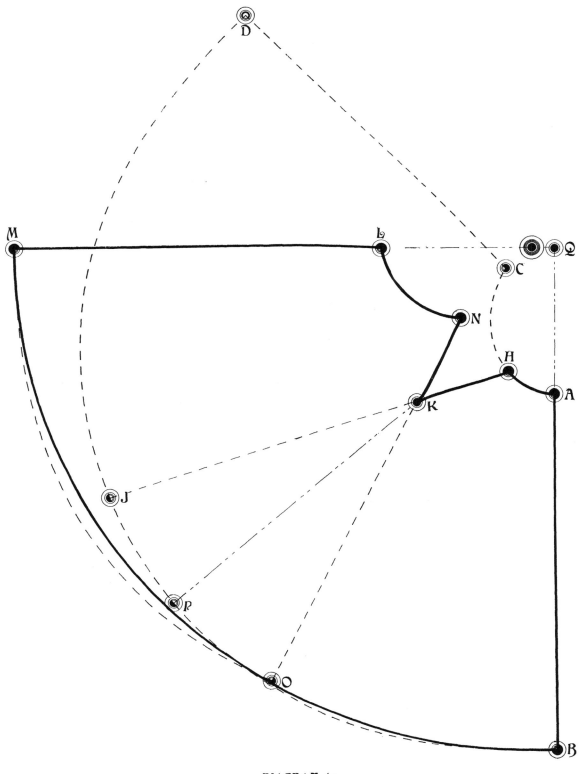

DIAGRAM 49.

HOOD.

DIAGRAM 50.

DRAW a straight line as from O to 3.

Lay the pattern of the back of the garment with which the hood is to be worn to touch the line ¼ inch below O, as at 1, and 1½ inch from the line at the waist, as from 3 to 4. The position of the back is shown in broken lines. Shape the top from O past 5 as represented.

Lay the pattern of the forepart as represented in broken lines with the shoulder-seam ½ inch from the back, and mark along the neck-gorge from 6 to the center-of-front at 7.

O to 2 is the length.

Square across from 2.

From 2 to 9 is according to the style effect desired.

Square up from 9.

From 9 to 8 is 3 inches for this draft.

Shape the front edge from 7 to 8 as represented.

O to 2 is cut on the fold of the goods. A hem is sometimes added to the front edge from 7 to 8, and a drawing string is inserted in the hem.

The light line extending from 7 to 10 shows a pointed hood, and that to 11 a round hood.

COLLARETTE HOOD.

DIAGRAM 51.

THE hood represented by this diagram has the effect of a collarette in front, the fold in the back extending only to the top of the shoulder. It is drafted in the following manner:

Draw a straight line as A 3.

Lay the pattern of the back of the coat on the paper with the center-back-seam touching the line at the top, and 1½ inch from the line at the natural waist as from 3 to 4.

From 1 to A is ¼ inch. Shape the gorge from A to 2.

A to B is two-thirds of the length of the hood, and A to C is the full length.

Pivot at A and sweep forward from B and C.

B to D is one-fourth of the full length of the hood. Draw a line from A through D to establish E.

From 1 to F is ⅓ bust, and F to G is 1 inch.

Lay the pattern of the forepart in the position shown by the broken lines, with point 6 ½ inch away from 2.

Shape the gorge from 2 to the lapel crease-line which is at H, or to the center-of-front as the case may be.

Shape the outer edge of the hood from H through G to E as represented.

B to 5 is half-way between B and C.

From A to 5 is cut on the fold of the goods, and the edges of the two sides are to be sewn together from D to E and D to 5.

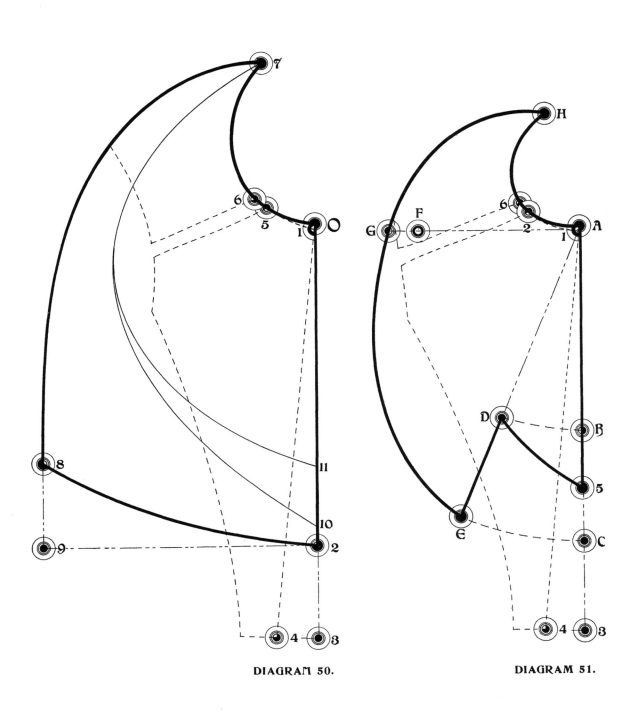

DIAGRAM 50.   DIAGRAM 51.

SMALL WAIST AND LARGE FRONT HIP.

DIAGRAM 52.

THIS diagram represents the forepart of a basque for a form which is very full over the front hips and small at the waist. An observation of the form when the measures were taken clearly showed that the largeness was at the *front*, and that the form was *flat at the sides*. The purpose is to show the adjustment of the quantity required on the front hip line.

The measures used are as follows : 6¾ back-scye depth, 14¾ length to natural waist, 10¾ blade, 12 front-scye depth, 15¾ over-shoulder, 6¾ back-waist, 11½ front hip, 40 bust, 26 waist, 48 hip.

TO DRAFT.

Proceed in the same manner as explained for Diagrams 1 and 2 for a waist, and as for Diagram 17 for a jacket, to establish the center-of-front line and points 1, 2, 3 and 4 on the waist line.

From 7 to 6 is ¼ inch less than from the middle of the first dart to 1.

From 10 to 9 is ¼ inch less than from the middle of the second dart to 3.

From 9 to 8 is ½ inch more than from 2 to 3.

Connect 1 and 6, 2 and 8, 3 and 9, and 4 and 10.

Q to Z is 1 inch less than the front hip.

Z to 5 is the front hip surplus, 2¾ inches for this draft.

Should the darts be drawn to the points already fixed on the hip line, viz., 6 to 8 and 9 to 10, the total amount taken out by the darts on the hip line would be 3¼ inches, which is one-half inch more than the front hip surplus, Z to 5. This ½ inch is distributed, one-half from 6 to X and one-half from 5 to Y.

Shape the center-of-front line below 25 towards Y, and the front edge of the first dart below 1 towards X.

In no case should the back edge of the second dart be drawn from 4 *forward of 10, and then only when the prominence is at the front of the abdomen.*

See Variations for the Front Hip.

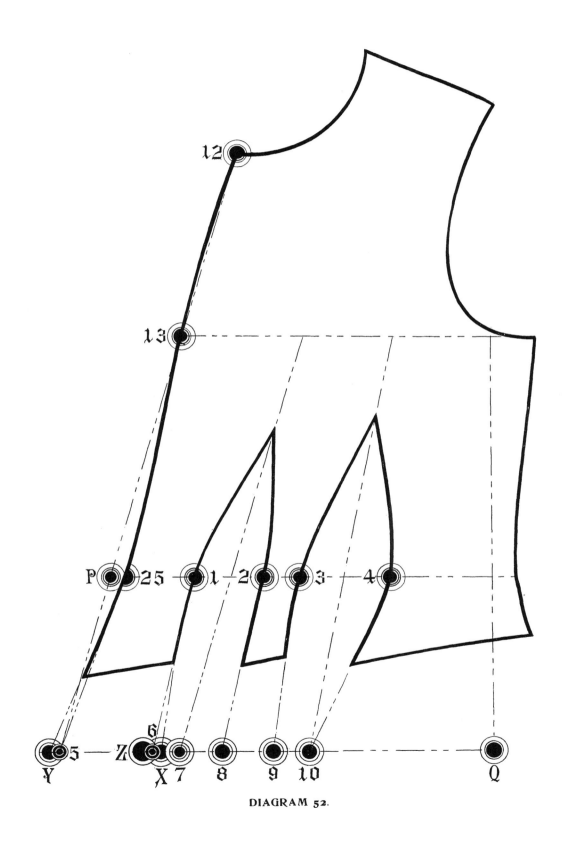

DIAGRAM 52.

CORPULENT FORMS.

DIAGRAM 53.

TWO changes are required when drafting for corpulent forms; one in the position of the front shoulder point N, and the other in the center-of-front line.

The diagram, which is drafted for a form that measures 42 bust, 34 waist, has two underarmpieces and a sidebody. Points G, H, T, P, 13 and 25 are obtained in the same manner as explained for all of the preceding coats which are less than tight-fitting through the fronts. (See Diagram 15.)

One-fourth of the back-waist surplus is taken out between T and 17, one-fourth between the two underarmpieces, one-fourth between the sidebody and next underarmpiece, and one-fourth between the sidebody and back.

To establish J and K we must now consider what is the degree of corpulency. For the average form we have 11 inches difference between the bust and waist circumferences. For the form which we are now considering, the difference between the bust and waist is but 8 inches. So we would say that it is 3 inches corpulent. The rule to be applied in such cases is as follows : *Establish J as many eighths of an inch back from H as the form is corpulent.* For this diagram, therefore, H to J is ⅜ inch.

Square up from J to establish N.

From 25 to K is one-third of the amount of corpulency. For this diagram, therefore, 25 to K is 1 inch.

The foregoing rule in relation to point J applies also to all garments which are to be made tight-fitting through the fronts.

T to 18 is the same as T to 17.

Place the back-waist quantity (which for this draft is 8 inches), at 18, and apply one-half of the full waist to establish V.

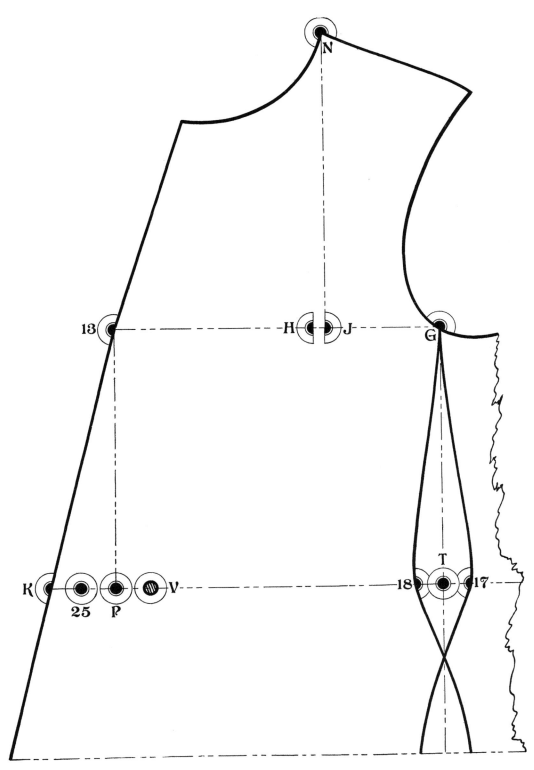

DIAGRAM 53.

SPREADING THE DARTS.

DIAGRAM 54.

FOR forms that are very full at the bust and small at the waist, a pattern drafted in the usual manner, excepting for forms which are small through the blade and have a small waist, will be *too short* over the brow of bust from the back of the neck to the waist line. The extreme prominence of the bust will draw the material up and cause fullness at the front of scye and directly opposite at the center-of-front.

To obviate this, extra length must be provided over the brow of bust. This is obtained by spreading the darts as is hereafter explained.

To determine whether additional length is required or not two measures are required: one from the back of the neck at the collar-seam, down close in front of scye to the waist line as at Q, and the other from the same point over the brow of bust midway between the front of scye and the center-of-front to the waist line *level with Q*, as from 1 through N to R.

These lengths will vary according to bust development. Whenever the difference between the two does not exceed 1 inch, no change is required to the original pattern, because the darts, if not less than 4 inches in width at the waist line, will give the additional 1 inch in length which is required.

Measure the width of the darts on the waist line. This we will suppose to be 4 inches. One-fourth of the width will be the extra over-bust length gained, which would be in this case 1 inch.

If, to illustrate, the over-bust length is 1¾ inch more than the side length, and the darts are 4 inches wide, then the *extra length* to be gained will be ¾ inch. In such case proceed as follows:

The line O P is the bust line.

Point 2 is half-way betwen O and P.

From 2 to 3 is the additional over-bust-length to be gained, which in this case is ¾ inch.

Lay the pattern of the forepart over another piece of paper and draw straight lines from P through 3 towards 4, and from O through 3 towards 5.

Mark along the edge of the pattern from N to O and N to P, and down on each side of the tongue between the darts as below S and T. Below the bust line the regular pattern is shown in broken lines.

Pivot at O and swing the lower part of the pattern back until the line O P is in line with O 5. Mark along the edge from O to 6, to 7, to 8, and up to the top of the dart, which, in the changed position of the pattern is now at 15.

Pivot at P and swing the lower part forward until the line O P is in line with P 4. Mark from P to 12, to 11, and up to the top of the dart, which is now at 14.

Remove the pattern.

Reshape the lines above 8 and 9 until they intersect not more than ¼ inch above T.

Reshape the lines above 10 and 11 until they intersect not more than ¼ inch above S.

Make the length from S to 10 the same as from S to 11, and that from T to 9 the same as T to 8.

Cut out the pattern as defined by the solid lines.

A small V should be taken out at the neck-gorge as represented.

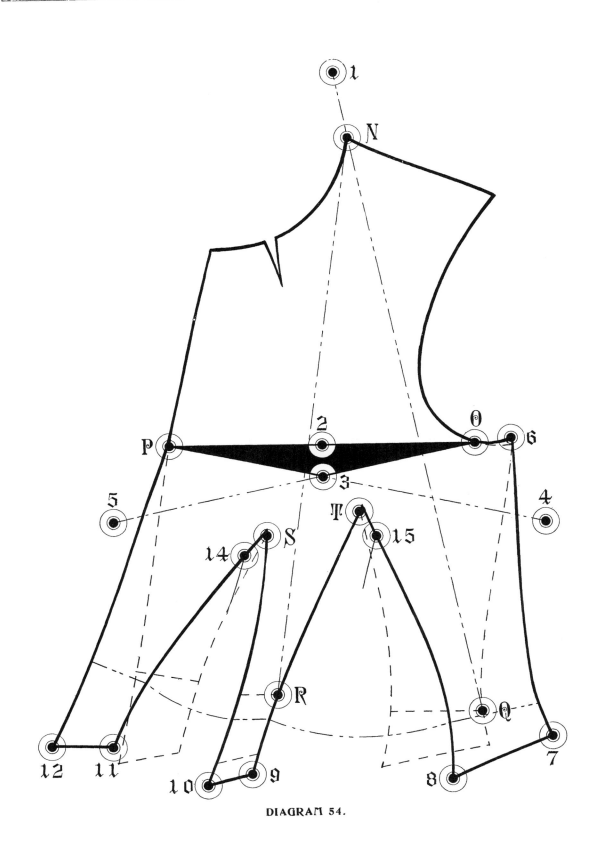

DIAGRAM 54.

VARIATIONS IN FRONT=OF=SCYE AND HALF=BACK WIDTH.

O N some of the diagrams in this work the front of scye is placed $\frac{1}{16}$ bust forward of the blade quantity as from G to 10 on Diagrams 1 and 5.

On others it is placed *less* than $\frac{1}{16}$ bust, as from G to 10 on Diagrams 15 and 21.

The method for obtaining the *proportionate* half-back width as shown on Diagrams 1 and 5 locates M on the top line $\frac{1}{16}$ bust from K, while on other diagrams from K to M is *less* than $\frac{1}{16}$ bust.

These seeming discrepancies are explained as follows :

The amount of fullness at the sleeve-head which is gathered or plaited into the scye, varies with changes in style. A sleeve with extreme fullness at the top can be better adjusted to a large armhole than to a small one. For which reason, when there is a large amount of fullness at the sleeve-head, G to 10 and K to M should each be $\frac{1}{16}$ bust.

When there is but a moderate amount of fullness to the top sleeve-head, a wider back and a smaller armhole is preferable to a large armhole and a narrow half-back. In which case G to 10 may be $\frac{1}{4}$ or $\frac{1}{2}$ inch less than $\frac{1}{16}$ bust, and for obtaining the proportionate half-back width, K to M may be $\frac{1}{4}$ or $\frac{1}{2}$ inch less than $\frac{1}{16}$ bust.

VARIATIONS IN THE FRONT HIP.

IT should be observed that on all diagrams for garments with backs close-fitting at the waist, from Q to Z on the hip line is *1 inch less than the front-hip measure.*

The reason for this seeming reduction of size through the front-hip is, that a part of the overlapping of the forepart and underarmpiece on each side of W (see Diagram 6), *becomes part of the front hip* when the underarm-seam is joined in making up. If, in addition to the amount gained in the overlap at W, the full hip measure was applied from Q to Z, there would be too much material through that part, and a corresponding deficiency at the side of the hip.

For the average form from Q to Z should therefore be about 1 inch less than the front-hip measure. This will increase the front-hip surplus from Z to 32 (see Diagrams 2 and 6), and widen the darts the same amount on the hip line. The application of the full hip measure distributes this 1 inch through the back-hip, two-thirds of it at the overlap at W and one-third at that at X.

Forms will frequently carry a large front-hip measure, but the prominence may be *at the side instead of being at the front as was explained for Diagram 52.* This must be observed when the measures are taken. When the prominence is at the front the darts should be drawn on the hip line as shown on Diagram 52. When it is at the side, from Q to Z should be 1½ to 1¾ inch less than the front hip measure. The center of front should be drawn to 5 as usual. The first dart should be drawn to 6 and 8 , and the back edge of the second dart will be ½ to ¾ inch back of 10, according to the extra amount which the front hip has seemingly been reduced.

SINGLE-BREASTED NO-COLLAR VEST.

DIAGRAM 55.

THE measures used for the accompanying diagram are as follows:

7 back-scye depth.	36 bust.
15¼ natural waist length.	25 waist.
10 blade.	10 opening.
11¼ front-scye depth.	13½ brow of bust.
15¼ over-shoulder.	19½ front-waist length.
6¼ back-waist.	23 front length.
9 front-hip.	

For all garments to be worn next to the corset cover the blade and back-waist measures are each reduced ¼ inch. These measures, as used when drafting, will therefore be 9¾ blade and 6 back-waist for this draft.

TO DRAFT.

Draw the line 1 D.

From 1 to A is $\frac{1}{24}$ bust. A to B is the back-scye depth. A to C is the length to the natural waist. C to D is 5½ inches. Square the cross lines from 1, B, C, and D.

C to E is 1½ inch for sizes above 36 bust. For less than 36 bust C to E is $\frac{1}{12}$ bust. Draw a straight line from A through E. This establishes F.

F to G is ¼ inch less than the blade measure, 9¾ inches for this draft. G to H is ½ inch more than ⅙ bust. F to 13 is half of the full bust. From 13 to I is ½ inch. Square up from H.

Square down from G to establish T and Q.

From 1 to L is ⅛ bust. Draw a straight line from L to I.

G to 8 is $\frac{1}{16}$ bust. Square up from 8.

L to 7 is ¾ inch less than ¼ bust. Shape the scye from 7 to the bust line as represented.

G to N is the front-scye depth less the width of the back A to L. Draw a line from N to G to establish R. N to K is ⅙ bust and L to J is the same.

F to J and G through R to K is the over-shoulder. Shape the shoulder seam from N through K, and make N to 6 the same as L to 7.

Point 2 is half-way between A and B. A line drawn from N to 2 will give the run of the front shoulder seam for the average form.

Square forward from N. N to O is ½ inch less than ⅙ bust. Draw a straight line from O through 13 to establish S on the hip line.

N to 12 is ½ inch less than ¼ bust. (Point 12 will be the height of the front for the average form for vests which are to close at the throat). Shape the center-

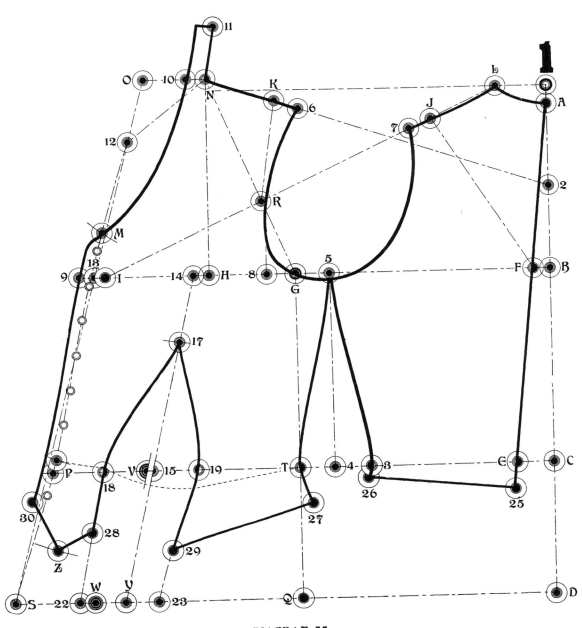

DIAGRAM 55.

of-front line from 12, passing ⅛ inch forward of 13 through P (which is ¼ inch back of the straight line 12 to S) and on to S as shown by the broken line.

E to 3 is ¼ inch less than the back waist measure, 6 inches for this draft.   3 to T represents the back waist surplus.

Establish 4 half-way between T and 3.   Square up from 4 to establish 5, and shape the underarm seam from 5 through 3 and from 5 through T, springing out sharply below T and 3.

From 3 to 26 is ½ inch, and T to 27 is 1½ inch.   Square back from 26 by the line A E to establish 25.

E to 3 and T to V is ¼ inch less than half of the full waist.

Point 14 is half-way between G and 13.   From T to 15 is 1 inch more than half-way between T and P.   Draw a line from 14 through 15 to establish Y.

From 15 to 18 is half of the quantity between V and P.   From 15 to 19 is the same as from 15 to 18.

A to L and N to 17 is the length to brow of bust.

Y to 22 is ¼ inch less than from 15 to 18.   Connect 18 and 22.

Q to W is 1 inch less than the front-hip.   W to S represents the front-hip surplus.   From 22 to 23 is the same as W to S.   Shape the dart as shown by the solid lines.

N to 10 is 1 inch.   N to 11 is the same as A to L.

From 11 through N to the sweep at M is the opening.   From 11 through N to the unlettered point just above P is the front waist length, and on to the sweep at Z is the front length.   Shape the opening through 10 and M, and add ½ inch below the opening for the front edge of the buttonhole front as from 9 to 30.   Space for the buttons.

Pivoting at 12, sweep back from the front waist length to the front edge of the dart.   From there sweep across the dart, pivoting at 17.   This waist line is shown by the broken line beginning just above P and extending back to the dart just above 18, then across the dart to just below 19.

Shape the lower front as from 30 to Z.   Cut out the dart and bring the sides of the dart to a closed position notch for notch, and shape the bottom edge from 27 to Z.   This will establish 28 and 29.

The back may be lengthened below E and 3 if so desired, as is shown on the succeeding diagram.   For forms with prominent hips it is preferable, however, that the backs be made short, as shown on this diagram.

Ladies' Calling
Toilette

Ladies' Tailor Suit

Ladies' Calling Toilette

The Delineator
May 1899

SINGLE=BREASTED VEST.

Notch Collar.

diagram 56.

THE measures used are the same as for the preceding diagram.

Points A, B, C, D, E, F, G, L, M, N, P, Q, S, T, W, 5, 6, 7, 9, 10, 11, 12, 13 and 30 are obtained in the same manner as explained for the preceding diagram.

E to U is ¼ inch less than the back-waist, 6 inches for this draft. U to 3 is 1 inch. Half-way between 3 and T establish 4. Square up from 4 to establish 5. Shape the underarm-seam from 5 through T, springing back sharply torward 27, also from 5 through 3, springing forward sharply toward 26.

T to 27 is 1½ inch for this draft, and 3 to 26 is the same.

From 3 to 1 is one-third of the distance between 3 and E. From 1 to 2 is the same as from U to 3. Shape the dart as represented. E to 25 is ½ inch more than from 3 to 26.

E to U and T to V is ¼ inch less than one-half of the full waist, and V to P is the front waist surplus—4 inches for this draft. This surplus is disposed of by the darts as follows:

P to 18 is 1¾ inch for this draft, but it may be made more or less according to taste or style. From 18 to 19 is ⅜ inch less than half of the front waist surplus, 1⅝ inch for this draft. From 19 to 20 is 1 inch. From 20 to 21 is the remainder of the front waist surplus, 2⅜ inches for this draft.

Divide the quantity between G and 13 into three equal parts to establish 14 and 15. Draw a straight line from a point ½ inch back of 14 down through the unlettered point which is half-way between 18 and 19. This establishes X.

Also draw a straight line from 15 down half-way between 20 and 21 to establish Y. N to 11 is the same as A to L.

From 11 through N to 17 is the length to brow of bust. Draw a line from F through 17 to establish 16.

To obtain the run of the waist apply the front waist length from 11 through N to the unlettered point just above P. Sweep back from this point to the front of the first dart, pivoting at 12, and thence across the dart, pivoting at 16. Extend the line across the tongue parallel with the line from 19 to 20, and from there back across the dart, pivoting at 17.

Make notches on this line at the darts.

From X to 22 is ¼ inch less than half the width of the first dart at the waist line. Connect 18 and 22.

From Y to 24 is ¼ inch less than half the width of the second and at the waist line. Connect 20 and 24.

From 24 to 23 is ½ inch more than from 19 to 20. Connect 20 and 24. Q to W is 1 inch less than the front hip. W to S is the front hip surplus. From 24 to 32 is the same as W to S less the amount taken out by the first dart from 22 to 23. Shape the darts as represented.

From 11 through N to M is the opening, and from 11 through N in a direct line to Z is the front length.

N to 10 is 1 inch. Shape the opening through 10 and M, and add ½ inch below the opening for the edge of the buttonhole front as from 9 to 30. Space for the buttonholes.

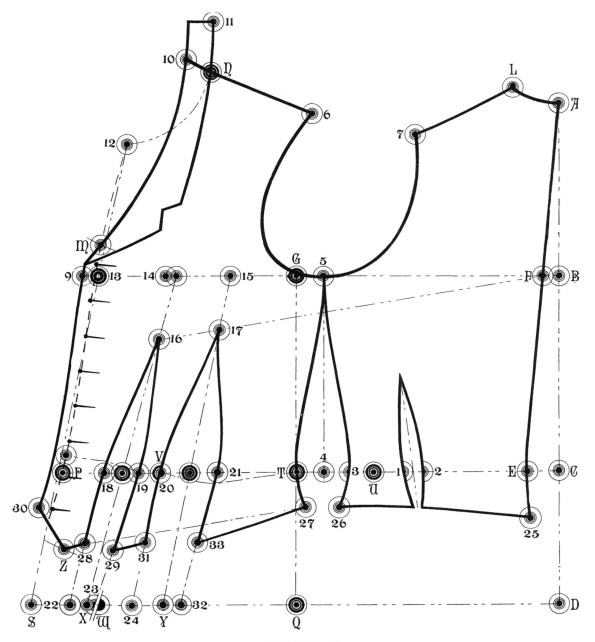

DIAGRAM 56.

Cut out the darts, bring the sides of the darts to a closed position notch for notch, and draw a straight line from Z to 27. This will establish 28, 29, 31 and 33.

THE COLLAR.—Lay the pattern of the front over another piece of paper and mark along the edge from 11 through 10 and M to the end of the collar. Remove the pattern and shape the leaf edge below 11 through N to taste or style.

The shoulder-seam of the front extends from 6 through N to 10.

The length of the back may be shortened below E and 3 as shown on the preceding diagram if so desired; in which case all of the quantity between T and U will be taken out by the underarm-cut, and the dart between 1 and 2 will be omitted.

DOUBLE=BREASTED VEST.

SEPARATE LAPELS. CREASED COLLAR.

DIAGRAM 57.

THE back may be drafted as explained for either of the two preceding diagrams.

Points N, 12, 13, P, and T are obtained in the same manner as explained for Diagram 55. The fronts may be drafted with single bust darts if desired, as explained for diagram 55.

Cut out the pattern of the forepart excepting the neck-gorge from N to 12.

THE LAPEL.

Lay the pattern of the forepart over another piece of paper and mark along the edge from 12 to Z, then to 28 and up the front edge of the first dart. Notch both parts as at A.

Cut out the lapel as thus far defined, and lay it in closing position with the forepart above the notches at A.

Establish the top buttonhole and space off for the remaining ones below.

N to E is 1 inch. Draw the lapel crease line from E to the top buttonhole at D.

Fold the upper part of the lapel on the crease line underneath the forepart. Shape the lapel according to style and with a tracing-wheel mark through on the paper which is underneath as from D to G and H.

Upon unfolding the paper the lapel will then be defined above D by points I and J. Shape the gorge from N to J as shown by the solid line.

THE COLLAR.

The intersection of the lapel crease line with the gorge establishes F. Draw the collar crease line from F through N. Make the stand 1 inch wide, and the seam edge J to 11, ¼ inch less than half of the full size of the gorge.

DOUBLE-BREASTED VEST. FLAT COLLAR.

DIAGRAM 58.

Points 10, 11, 12, 13, 28, N, P and T are obtained in the same manner as explained for Diagram 55. The fronts may be drafted with single bust darts if desired, except for forms which are very small at the waist in proportion to the bust size, as explained for Diagram 55.

THE LAPEL.

Having first cut out the forepart on the center-of-front line, lay it over another piece of paper, and mark along the lapel edge from 12 to Z, then to 28 and up along the front of the first dart. Notch both parts at or near 13.

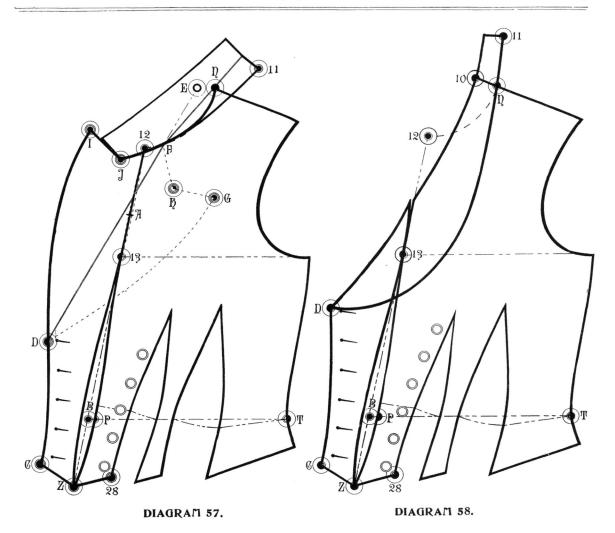

DIAGRAM 57.   **DIAGRAM 58.**

Cut out the lapel as thus far defined, and lay it in a closing position with the forepart above the notches at 13.

Establish the top buttonhole and space for the remaining ones below.

Shape the opening from D through 10 as represented.

THE COLLAR.

Lay the pattern of the forepart and lapel over another piece of paper in closing position above the notches, and mark along the edge from 11 through 10 to D. Remove the patterns and cut the shoulder-seam of the forepart through N to 10.

Shape the free edge of the collar to taste or style.

WHOLE FRONTS.

These vests are sometimes made with whole fronts or without the lapel-seam. In such cases fold the pattern of the forepart on the straight line from 12 through B to Z. Then mark along the edge of the pattern from Z to 28 and up along the front of the first dart. Now unfold the paper and proceed as already explained.

NOTE.—It must be distinctly observed that for the *creased* collar, as shown on Diagram 57, the front shoulder point is at N, while for the *flat* collar as shown on Diagrams 56 and 58, it is at 10.

The Delineator
March 1902
Ladies' Seven-Gored Skirt with Flounce

Ladies'
Mackintosh
Coat

Ladies' Empire
Long Coat

Ladies'
Long Coat

The Designer
February 1902

SKIRTS.

———

THE measures required are the waist, taken snug; the hip taken easy and about 5½ inches below the waist, front, side and back lengths each taken to the floor. The lengths can be changed to the fashionable lengths when drafting the skirt.

Unless the waist line is clearly defined, it will be advantageous to place an elastic band or a strap around the waist. The bottom of the band should be at the bottom of the waist *at the sides*, and from there should be made *level* to the center of the back. From the sides to the front it should follow the natural run of the waist line.

The lengths should be taken close to the form at the bottom independent of any additional back length for train.

DIAGRAM 59.

On this diagram are shown seven skirts of differing degrees of fullness at the waist-line and of size around the bottom.

The center-of-back is defined, for the first, by the broken line extending upward from D1, and for the others by the lines extending upward from 1, 2, 3, 4, 5 and 6.

Each skirt will lie plain about the hips, but with different degrees of fullness at the sides and back below the hip, and with different degrees of fullness at the waist line. The fullness at the waist may be disposed of either by darts, or it may be shrunk on to the band according to the amount of fullness.

To obtain the different degrees of fullness at the sides, six sweeping points are shown on the diagram. Nos. 1, 2 and 3 are on the line which is extended upwards above B, and Nos. 4, 5 and 6 on the line above F.

When it is desired that a skirt shall hang plain around the bottom at the sides, sweeping point No. 1 should be used. If less plain, No. 2 should be used, and so on. A glance at the diagram will show the several curvations at the waist, hip and bottom produced by the use of these six sweeping-points. Additional size may be given around the bottom of gored skirts by overlapping the lines which define the width of the gores at the bottom; by plaits at the bottom of each gore-seam, and by circular flounces as shown on subsequent diagrams. In such case, if it is desired that the skirt shall hang plain about the sides above the flare which is thus given at the bottom, the sweeping-point No. 1 should be used.

The system is applicable to every size of waist and hip, and the seams may be located to suit the width of the material used.

*　　　*　　　*

The skirt No. 2 shown on this diagram is defined by points A B, and 1 on the waist, hip and bottom lines.

A to B is the front length.

B to C is 5½ inches.

B to 3 is the full waist, and from 3 to 1 is one-half of the full waist.

Pivot at 1 and sweep backwards from B, C and A.

C to 1 on the hip line is one-half of the full hip.

A to D1 is the full hip.

D1 to 1 at the left is ½ hip on the divisions of halves, or one-fourth of the full hip.

Draw a straight line from 1 at the bottom through 1 on the hip line. This establishes 1 on the waist line.

The skirt No. 3 is defined by points A, B and 2 on the waist, hip and bottom lines.

B to 3 is the full waist, and from 3 to 2 is one-fourth of the full waist.

Pivot at 2 and sweep backward from B, C and A.

C to 2 on the hip line is one-half of the full hip.

A to D2 is the full hip.

D2 to 2 at the left is ½ hip on the divisions of Halves and Fourths, or three-eights of the full hip.

Draw a straight line from 2 at the bottom through 2 on the hip line. This establishes 2 on the waist line.

*   *   *

The skirt No. 4 is defined by A, B and 3 on the waist, hip and bottom lines.

B to 3 is the full waist.

Pivot at 3 and sweep backward from B, C and A.

C to 3 on the hip line is one-half of the full hip.

A to D3 is the full hip.

D3 to 3 at the left is one-half of the full hip.

Draw a straight line from 3 at the bottom through 3 on the hip line. This establishes 3 on the waist line.

*   *   *

The skirt No. 5 is defined by points A, B and 4 on the waist, hip and bottom lines.

C to E is ½ waist on the divisions of fourths, or one-eighth of the full waist. Draw a line up from E parallel with the line C3. This establishes F.

F to 4 is one-half of the full waist.

F to 6 is one-fourth of the full waist.

Half-way between 4 and 6 establish 5.

Pivot at 4 and sweep backwards from F, E and A.

C to 4 on the hip-line is one-half of the full hip.

Draw a straight line from midway between 5 and 6 through 4 on the hip line. This establishes 4 at the bottom.

*   *   *

The skirt No. 6 is defined by points A, B and 5 on the waist, hip and bottom lines.

Pivot at 5 above F and sweep backwards from F, E and A.

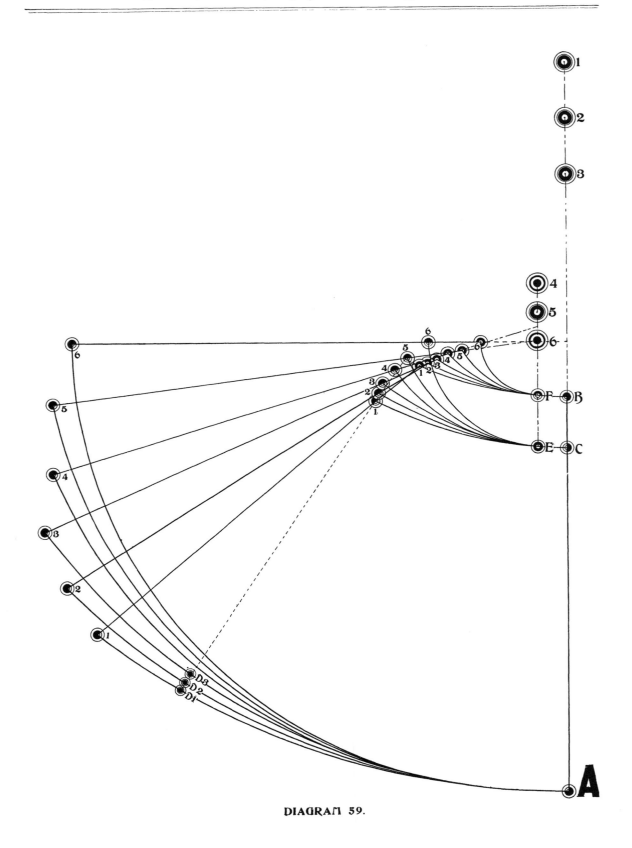

DIAGRAM 59.

C to 5 on the hip line is one-half of the full hip.

Draw a straight line from 6 above F through 5 on the hip line. This establishes 5 at the bottom.

*　　　*　　　*

The skirt No. 7 is defined by points A, B and 6 on the waist, hip and bottom lines.

Pivot at 6 above F and sweep backwards from F, E and A.

C to 6 on the hip line is one-half of the full hip.

Square back by the line A B through 6 on the hip line. This establishes 6 at the bottom.

A line drawn from D1 through 1 on the hip-line would define a very close skirt (the smallest which should be made).

The manner of disposing of the surplus of size on the waist-line by shrinking or by darts, and for the application of varying front, side and back lengths, is given in the explanations of the succeeding diagrams.

These skirts may be made gored or circular as desired.

GENERAL NOTES ON SKIRTS.

———

BY a gored skirt is meant one which has one or more seams on each side. A circular skirt is without seams at the sides.

A one-piece skirt is of course cut circular, with but one seam which may be placed at the center-of-back or at the front. (Diagram 68.)

A two-piece skirt is usually made with a narrow front gore. The back is laid with the center-of-back on a fold of the material. It can be made with a wide front gore if desired by placing the seam below the middle dart.

A three-gored skirt has one front and two back gores.

A four-gored skirt has one front, 2 side, and one back gore. The back gore is cut with the center-of-back laid on a fold of the material.

A five-gored skirt has one front, two side, and two back gores. (Diagrams 60 and 62.)

A six-gored skirt has one front, two side, two side-back and one back gore. The center-of-back is laid on a fold of the material.

A seven-gored skirt has one front, two side, two side-back and two back gores. (Diagram 69.)

A nine-gored skirt has one front, two side-front, two side, two side-back and two back gores.

For a nine-gored skirt one full fourth of the waist surplus is taken out at the top of each gore seam. Each of the gores on the waist line is one-fifth of a full half of the waist in width.

An eleven-gored skirt has one front, two side-front, four side, two side-back and two back gores.

For an eleven-gored skirt a full one-fifth of the waist surplus is taken out at the top of each gore seam. Each of the gores on the waist line is one-sixth of a full half of the waist in width.

Wash skirts should be cut six gores. The front may be the same as shown on Diagram 60. The front edge of the back-gore should be drawn below the third dart to G (Diagram 60). This gives less bias to that edge. The seam below the middle dart should be drawn to a point 2 inches less than half-way from 1 to G. Add 2½ to 3 inches back of I for gathers. The waist line should be raised back of 9 when the fullness is to be gathered to the waist. By pivoting 4 inches below D and sweeping back from 9 will give about the proper change in the run of the waist line across the gathers.

For skirts other than wash skirts, any amount may be added for gathers back of I according to style and the nature of the material used. In any case all that part which is back of 9 is to be gathered to equal the quantity between 9 and I.

FIVE=GORED SKIRT. (Three Darts.)

Single Underfolding Box Plait.

DIAGRAM 60.

ON this diagram a skirt is represented that will hang plain around the hips and sides. To obtain this effect sweeping-point No. 1 as explained for the preceding diagram is used.

The measures used are 24 waist, 42 hip, 42 front, side and back lengths.

TO DRAFT.

Draw a line as A E.

A to C is the front length. C to B is 5½ inches. C to D is the full waist 24 inches. D to E is one-half of the full waist, 12 inches. Pivot at E and sweep back from A B and C.

B to F is one-half of the full hip, 21 inches.

A to 1, 1 to 2, 2 to 3, 3 to G and G to H are each ½ hip on the divisions of halves, or one-fourth of the full hip, 10½ inches. Draw a straight line from H through F to establish I.

By measuring along the sweep-line from C to I we find that we have 16 inches for this draft. As one-half of the full waist is but 12 inches, 16 inches is 4 inches too much. This 4 inches is taken out by the darts as follows :

C to 4 is ½ waist on the divisions of fourths, or ⅛ of the full waist. From 4 to 5 is one-fourth of the waist surplus, 1 inch for this draft. From 5 to 6 is the same as C to 4. From I to 9 is the same as C to 4. From 9 to 8 is the same as from 4 to 5. From 8 to 7 is the same as C to 4. This leaves one-half of the waist surplus, 2 inches for this draft, from 6 to 7.

Draw straight lines from midway between 4 and 5 to 1, and from midway between 8 and 9 to 3. Draw a short line from midway between 6 and 7 towards 2 for the run of the second dart. Shape the darts as represented.

H to K is the width desired for a plait, say 12 inches. Square up from K towards L. K to L is approximately 4 inches. The exact position of L is obtained later.

I towards J is 3 inches. Connect I and L.

Cut out the pattern, getting rid of as much superflous paper as possible, but leaving a margin at the top above 9 to J, and at the bottom below 3 and K.

Fold the shaded part underneath on the center-of-back line H I. Then fold it in the reverse way bringing the edge J L directly under the line H I. This gives the underfold which is represented by the line from 10 to 11.

When thus folded the shaded portion will all lie forward of the line H I. Now cut across the folds on the line from 9 to I. Apply the back-length from I to M and cut across the folds on the line from M to the side-length at 3. On opening out the folds the top will be as shown by the solid line I, 10, J, and the bottom by the broken line L M. Shorten the underfold ½ inch as to 11.

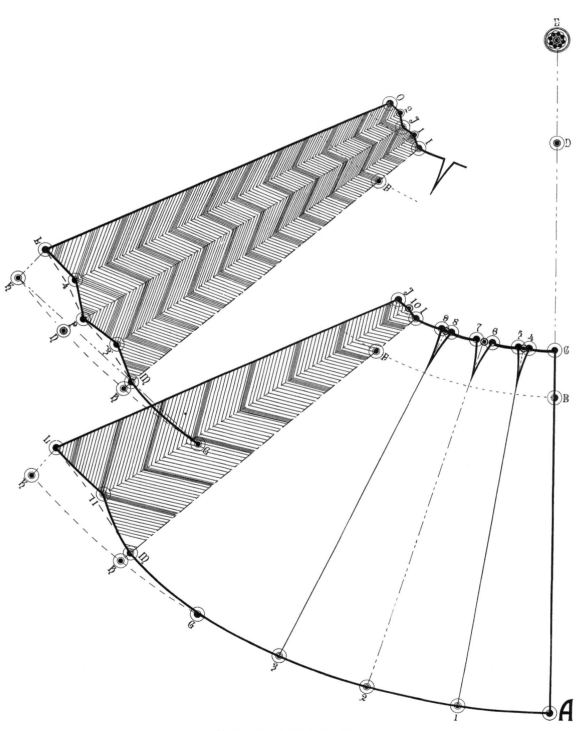

DIAGRAMS 60 AND 61.

The plait may be made an outward box-plait by changing the first fold (line H I) so that the plait will lie on top instead of underneath the body of the skirt. In which case the length at the bottom of the plait will be on the line L M.

DOUBLE-UNDERFOLDING-PLAIT.

DIAGRAM 61.

Points I, F, G, H and M are obtained in the same manner as for the preceding diagram

H to K is 16 inches. Square up from K. K to L is approximately 6 inches. P is half-way from L to M.

I to O is 6 inches and O is about 3 inches above the sweep-line from A which is shown below O in a broken line. The exact positions of O and L are obtained after the plaits are folded.

Cut the paper on the line O L. Leave a margin of paper across the top from the third dart to O, and across the bottom from G to K.

J is half-way from I to O.

As an aid in forming the plaits run a tracing-wheel along the lines I H, and J N.

Turn the pattern over and fold the paper forward, on the line J N, then by a reverse fold bring the line O L even with the fold J N. This gives the underfold below 2. Now fold the paper forward on the line I H, then by a reverse fold bring the line J N even with the fold I H. This gives the underfold below 1.

When the plaits are thus folded all of the shaded part will lie over the part which is not shaded. Now turn the pattern over and cut across the folded part on the waist-line from the third dart to I, and at the bottom forward of M to nothing at the side length.

On unfolding the plaits the top will be as represented by the solid line from I to O, and the bottom by the broken line from L through P.

Re-shape the bottom through 3 and 4 which are each ½ inch above the broken line.

The Delineator
May 1899

**Ladies' Six-Piece Skirt
with Slight Drapery
Gathers at the Back**

Ladies' Cycling Costume

FIVE=GORED SKIRT. (Two Darts.)

OUTWARD BOX-PLAIT EACH SIDE OF THE CENTER-BACK SEAM.

DIAGRAM 62.

THE body of the skirt is designed for forms having a large waist in proportion to hip size. The surplus on the waist line is disposed of by two darts instead of three as is shown on the preceding diagram. It will hang plain at the sides.

The measures used are 27 waist, 42 hip, 42 front, side and back lengths.

TO DRAFT.

Draw a straight line as A E.

A to C is the front length. C to B is 5½ inches. C to D is the full waist. D to E is one-half of the full waist.

Pivot at E (which corresponds with sweeping-point 1 on Diagram 59), and sweep back from B, C and A. B to F is one-half of the full hip.

A to G is the full hip. G to H is ½ hip on the divisions of halves or one-fourth of the full hip. Draw a straight line from H through F. This establishes I.

Measure along the sweep-line from C to I. For this draft C to I is 16½ inches, 3 inches more than one full half the waist required. This 3 inches is taken out by the darts as follows.

C to 4 is ½ waist on the divisions of thirds, or ⅙ of the full waist. From 4 to 5 is one-third of the waist surplus (1 inch for this draft). From 5 to 6 is the same as C to 4. From I to 7 is the same as C to 4. This leaves two-thirds of the waist surplus from 6 to 7, 2 inches for this draft.

A to 2 is one-fourth of the full hip. From 2 to 3 is 2 inches less than half-way from 2 to H. Draw straight lines from midway between 4 and 5 to 2, and from midway between 6 and 7 to 3. Shape the darts as represented.

I to M is the back length. I to X is 12 inches. Pivot at X and sweep back from I towards J, and from M towards L.

I to 8, 8 to 9, and 9 to J are each whatever is desired for the make up width of the plait at the waist-line which for this draft is 2 inches.

From M to 11, 11 to 12 and 12 to L are each 9 inches or as much as desired for the plait. 10 is half-way between 9 and J, and 13 is half-way between 12 and L. Connect 8 and 11, 9 and 12, 10 and 13, and J and L as represented.

Cut out the pattern leaving a margin of paper across the top from 7 to J, and from 3 to L at the bottom.

Run a tracing-wheel along the lines from H to I, 8 to 11, and 9 to 12.

The shaded parts are folded underneath. That part which is not shaded is the top side of the plait. The line H I is the underfold for the side of the plait. The line from 8 to 11 folds forward to the dotted line below 14. This brings the line from 9 to 12 directly on the line H I. The line from 10 to 13 is the underfold of the back of the plait. The shaded part between 9 and J folds underneath the un-shaded part from 8 to 9.

When the plait is thus folded, it will all lie on top of the pattern forward of the line H I. Cut across the folds from 7 to I. When opened out, the top of the plait will be shaped from I to J as represented.

Shape the bottom from the side-length at 3 through M to L, dropping about 2 inches below the sweep-line midway between 11 and 12.

A seam may be placed on the line I M if desired.

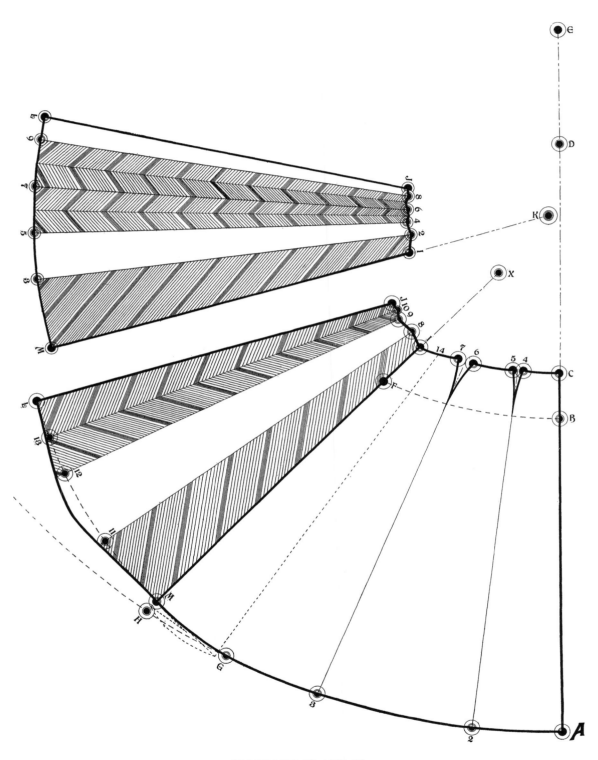

DIAGRAMS 62 AND 63.

Five=Gored Skirt. (Two Darts.)

(Continued.)

BOX-PLAIT AT BACK CENTER AND ONE EACH SIDE.

DIAGRAM 63.

The line I M corresponds to the line I M on the preceding diagram.

I to K is 16 inches.

Pivot at K and sweep back from I towards J, and from M towards L.

I to 2 is one and a half times the width of the face of the plait. In this instance the finished width of each plait is to be 1½ inch at the waist; so I to 2 is 2¼ inches.

From 2 to 4 is the finished width of the plait, 1½ inch for this diagram.

From 4 to 6 and 6 to 8 are the same as 2 to 4.

From 8 to J is one-half the width of the plait, ¾ inch.

M to 3 is 8¾ inches (or one-and-a-half times the width of the face of the plait, which is to be 5½ inches).

From 3 to 5, 5 to 7, and 7 to 9 are each 5½ inches.

From 9 to L is 2¾ inches, or one-half of the width from 3 to 5. Connect 2 and 3, 4 and 5, 6 and 7, 8 and 9 and J and L.

Cut the pattern on the line J L and leave a small margin of paper across the top from I to J, and across the bottom M to L.

Run a tracing-wheel along the lines below I, 2, 4 and 8.

The line from 8 to 9 folds forward to the line from 6 to 7. The line from 4 to 5 folds backward to the line from 6 to 7. The line from 2 to 3 folds forward to the dotted line below 14 on the preceding diagram.

A seam may be placed on the line I M.

The line J L, which is at the middle of the center plait, should be cut on the fold of the material.

Ladies' Coat

Ladies' Toilette

The Designer
February 1902

OUTWARD DOUBLE BOX=PLAIT.

ROUND AND TRAIN LENGTHS.

DIAGRAM 64.

THE shaded part represents the plait. It is drafted as follows:

Points A, B, C, D, E, F, G, H, I and 3 are obtained in the same manner as explained for diagram 60.

I to O is 4 inches. Observe that O is about 2½ inches above the sweep-line from C. The exact position is determined later on.

H towards P is 22 inches, or less if desired.

Draw a straight line from P up through O towards X, and extend the line H I up to establish X. I to M is the back length. Pivot at X and sweep back from I, also sweep forward and backward from M. This establishes L.

The line L M G represents the round length.

On the diagram an added length of 4 inches for a train is given from M to Q. Shape the bottom from A to Q as represented, and get rid of as much of superfluous paper as possible by cutting out all of the parts, leaving a margin of paper across the top, back of the third dart, and across the bottom back of Q.

I to J is 2½ inches. H to N is about 2 inches more than one-half of the quantity between H and P.

To make the folds easily, first run a tracing-wheel along the lines I, Q and J, N.

Fold the shaded part forward on the line J N, and then by a reverse fold backward bringing the line O P directly over the line J N. This gives the underfold from 2 to 6.

Next fold all of the shaded part forward on the center-of-back line I Q, and then by a reverse fold bring the line J N directly over the line I Q. This gives the underfold 1 to 5.

When thus folded all of the shaded part will lie over the part not shaded. Point 1 will be over 7, and 2 over 8.

Cut across the folds at the top from the third dart to I, and at the bottom on the solid line forward of Q.

When the plait is unfolded it will be as defined by the solid line from I to O at the waist, and Q to P at the bottom.

The center of the plait, which is represented by the line O P, may be cut on the fold of the material. In which case a seam may be placed on the line I Q.

As many seams as may be required may be placed on the part forward of the line I Q, or it may be cut circular.

HABIT BACK.

DIAGRAM 65.

THE back finish is without plaiting or fullness at the waist and hips. The center-of-back line may be continued in a straight line from I to H or spring out at the bottom as represented. When cut as represented, the added bottom fullness will display itself in graceful folds below the hip-line in the back. The back-seam should be stretched up and down at, and just below F.

TO DRAFT.

Points F, G, H and I are obtained as for the preceding diagrams.

Apply the back-length from I towards H. Pivot at F and sweep backward from the back-length towards L for round length.

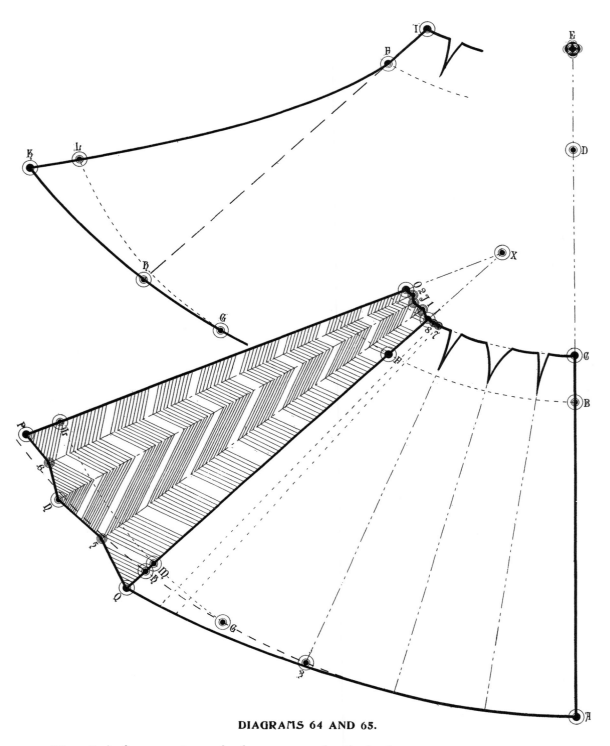

DIAGRAMS 64 AND 65.

H to L is from 15 to 20 inches as may be desired.

Add 2 to 6 or 8 inches as may be required from L to K for train length, and shape the bottom from K to the side-length as represented.

Shape the center-back-seam from I through F to L or K as represented.

SKIRT WITH FLOUNCE.

DIAGRAM 66.

THE skirt is first drafted full length to any desired style. For this diagram all forward of the line I H, except the flounce, is drafted as explained for Diagram 60. The part back of the line I H, is drafted as explained per Diagram 65.

Flounces are made in all varieties of shape, which must be determined by the current style.

To produce the flounce outline the top edge to the desired shape as from 5 to 10, and cut off the part below which is defined by points A, K, 10 and 5.

Take this part and lay it over another piece of paper. Mark along the edge of the paper from A to 1, A to 5, and 5 to 6.

From 1 to S is 1½ inch, more or less as required. Pivot at 6 and swing the lower part from 1 to S. Mark along the edge of the pattern from S to 2 and from 6 to 7. This gives 11.

From 2 to T is 2 inches, more or less as required. Pivot at 11 and swing the lower part from 2 to T. Mark from T to 3 and from 7 to 8. This gives 12.

From 3 to U is 2 inches, more or less as required. Pivot at 12 and swing the lower part from 3 to U. Mark from U to G and from 8 to 9. This gives 13.

From G to V 2½ inches more or less as required. Pivot at 13 and swing the lower part from G to V. Mark from 9 to 10 and from G to K. This gives 15 and W.

The flounce is defined by the part which is shaded.

The amount of each spread as from 1 to S, 2 to T, etc., depends upon the extra width required around the bottom of the flounce which is to be determined by the style effect to be produced. It is largely a matter of judgment, but the effect of the several spreads can be sufficiently ascertained after the flounce has been shaped, by placing a weight on the upper part of the skirt and securing the upper edge of the flounce by pins driven at short intervals along the lower edge of the upper part. If too much length has been gained at the lower edge of the flounce, take another piece of paper, repeat the operation as above explained lessening the amount of each spread. If more size is desired at the bottom increase each spread.

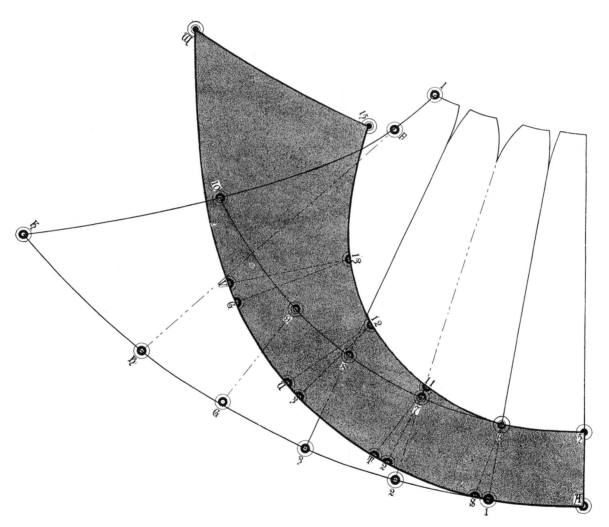

DIAGRAM 66.

TUNIC.

DIAGRAM 67.

THE underskirt shown on this diagram is the same as the body of the one shown on the preceding diagram. The tunic is defined by the part which is shaded. It may be applied to any style of skirt, gored or circular.

Having first defined the lower edge of the tunic to taste or to the prevailing style as between Y and Z, lay the pattern of the underskirt over another piece of paper.

Mark the lower edge of the tunic by a tracing-wheel.

Shape the waist-line of the tunic the same as that of the underskirt.

The front and back of the tunic may be shaped to correspond with the center-of-front and the center-of-back of the underskirt, or to taste or style.

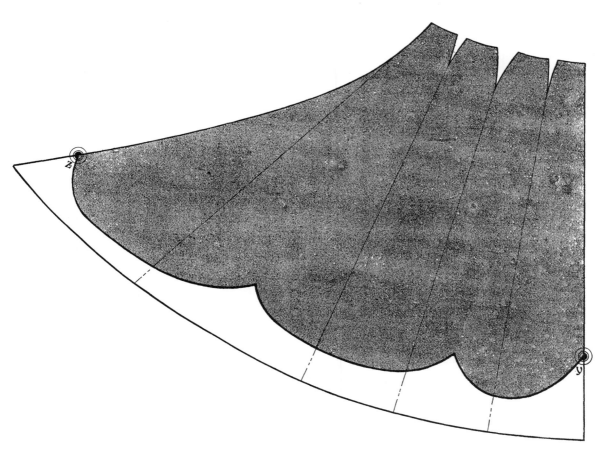

DIAGRAM 67.

CIRCULAR SKIRT.

DIAGRAM 68.

THIS skirt will hang plain around the front, but will be fuller around the bottom at the sides than those shown on the preceding diagram because of the curve given to the waist-line back of J. It is fitted plain about the hips and is without fullness at the back-waist. Whatever fullness there may be on the waist-line is either shrunk on to the band as between W and X, or taken out by a dart as preferred. The line A C is the center-front. The two fronts overlap each other, the right over the left, as from A to R.

THE DRAFT.

Draw a straight line as E C.

A to B is 5½ inches, and A to C is the front length.

A to D is the full waist, and D to E is half of the full waist.

Pivot at E and cast short sweeps from A, B and C.

A to J is ½ waist on the divisions of fourths or ⅛ of the full waist, and B to I is the same.

Draw a straight line from I through J.

J to K is one-half of the full waist.

L is half-way from J to K.

M is half-way from K to L.

N is half-way from L to M.

Pivot at K (which corresponds to sweeping-point 4 on Diagram 59), and cast sweeps from I, J and from the front length opposite C.

B to F following the sweep-line is one-half of the full hip.

Draw a straight line from N through F to establish O and P.

Apply the back length from O towards P. The length as to P is round length.

P to Q is as much as is desired for added train length. Shape the bottom to either point as represented.

A to W is one-fourth of the full waist, or ½ waist on the divisions of halves. O to X is the same as A to W.

W to X represents the surplus on the waist-line which may be shrunk to the band, or taken out by darts as shown on Diagram 62. If shrunk to the band the waist-line should be raised a trifle above the sweep-line at the prominence of the hips as shown by the solid line drawn above the broken line at W and X.

A to R and C to S represents the overlap at the center-of-front.

Any style of plaiting may be added back of the line O Q as required. When the opening is in front, as in this case, the back center may be laid on the fold of the material.

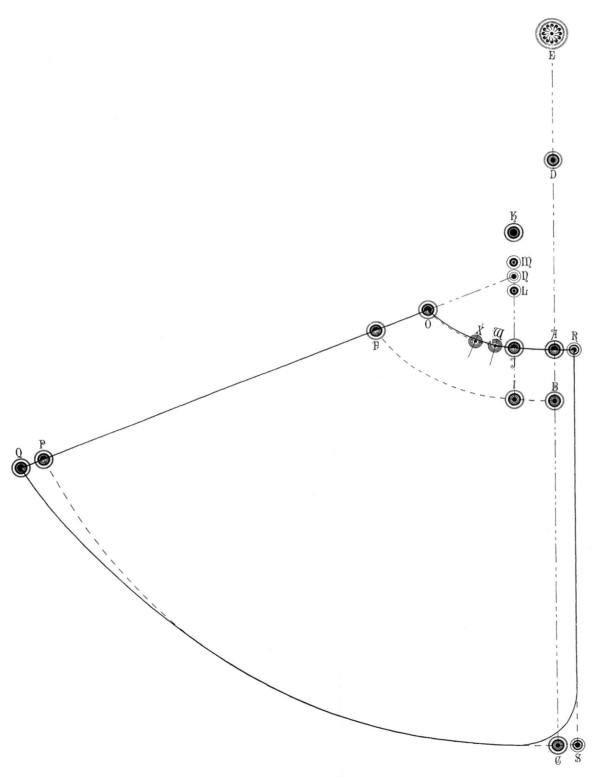

DIAGRAM 68.

SKIRT WITH YOKE.

DIAGRAM 69.

THIS skirt will lie plain around the hips. It will be moderately close at the knees, with a moderate degree of flare at the bottom. It is fitted to the waist by darts which are concealed by a circular yoke. The back finish is an underfolding box-plait and side plait on each side. The measures used are the same as for Diagram 60.

TO DRAFT.

Points A, B, C, D, E, F, G, H, I, 4, 5, 6, 7, 8 and 9 are obtained in the same manner as explained for Diagram 60.

A1 is half-way between A and C. Sweep from A1, pivoting at E. This establishes W on the center-of-back line.

A1 to X is one-half and one-fourth of the full hip.

X to W represents the amount to be taken out on the gore seams as follows: one-third between 10 and 11, one-third between 12 and 13, and one-third between 14 and 15. If it is required that the skirt shall be closer about the knees, make from A1 to X one-half and one eighth of the full hip.

For a five-gored skirt two-thirds of the quantity from X to W is taken out from 14 to 15, and the overlap at 3 should include the amount which is lost at 2 by omitting the seam above. A to 1 is 1 inch less than one-fourth of the full hip.

From 1 to 2 is 1 inch more than one-fourth of the full hip.

From 2 to 3 is 3 inches more than one-fourth of the full hip. From 1 to Q and 1 to R are each 1 inch. From 2 to S and 2 to T are each 1½ inch. From 3 to U and 3 to V are each 2 inches.

THE PLAITS.

H to K is 1½ inch. Connect I and K. I to M is the back length.

M in the direction of N is the width desired for the side-plait, say 6 inches.

N towards P is the same as H to K. P towards L is 3 inches more than M to N. I to O is from 4 to 6 inches.

Draw a line from L through O and extend the line above I until it intersects the line L O as at 18. Pivot at 18 and sweep back from I and M. Re-establish the widths from I to O, M to N, P and L *on the sweep lines*. J is half-way between I and O. Connect J and N, J and P, and O and L. Run a tracer along the lines I M and J P.

All the shaded parts when plaited lie underneath. The line I M is the first fold, and is folded backward over the line J N. This gives the underfold line above Z. The line J P is the second fold, and is folded backward over the line O L. This gives the underfold line above Y.

When the plaits are thus folded, cut across the top on the line from 9 to I, and across the bottom from opposite the back length at M to the side length at 2. On unfolding the plaits the top and bottom will be as defined by the solid lines I to O, and M to L.

THE YOKE.

B to E1 is one-half of the waist on the divisions of fourths, or one-eighth of the full waist. C to D1 is the same as B to E1. Draw a straight line from E1 up through D1. D1 to B4 is one-half of the full waist. B6 is half-way between B4 and D1. B5 is half-way between B4 and B6.

Pivot at B5 and sweep backward from D1 and E1. (B4, B5, and B6 correspond respectively with the sweeping points 4, 5 and 6 on Diagram 59.)

B following the sweep line to F1 is the same as B to F. (One-half of the full hip.) Draw a straight line from B6 to F1. This establishes 17.

By measuring from C to 17 we find that we have for this diagram 12¾ inches. This is ¾ inch more than one-half of the full waist, which must be shrunk on to the band over the fullest part of the hip.

Should the material be of such nature that fullness cannot well be shrunk on to the band, or if less fullness is desired, use B6 as the sweeping-point instead of B5. Then establish F1 as before explained, and square forward from F1 by the center-of-front line to establish 17. (See Diagram 59.)

The bottom of the yoke may be made pointed at each gore seam if preferred, or in any shape desired.

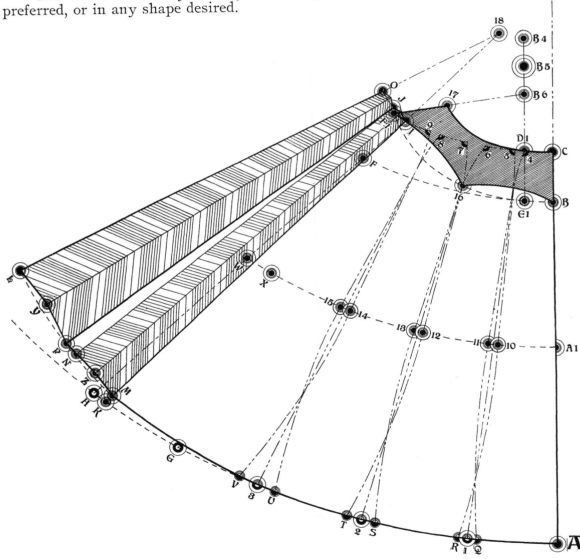

DIAGRAM 69.

DIVIDED SKIRT.

(BICYCLE.)

DIAGRAM 70.

THE measures used for the draft on the opposite page are as follows : 11¼ rise, 33 length, 23 waist, 40 hip.

The rise is taken, when the lady is seated, from the waist to the top of the chair seat.

Draw the line A B.   B to C is the length, 33 inches for this draft.   C to D is 5½ inches.   C to A is the full waist, 23 inches.   (A corresponds with sweeping point No. 3 on Diagram 59).

Sweep from C, D and B, pivoting at A.

D to E, following the sweep, is one-half the full hip, 20 inches for this draft.

B to F is one-fourth of full hip, 10 inches for this draft, or ½ hip on the division of halves on the ordinary tailor's square.

F to G, G to H and H to I are each the same as B to F.

Draw a straight line from I up through E.   This locates J.

Measure the quantity from C to J and from this deduct one-half of the full waist.   This leaves 4½ inches for this draft which is to be taken out by the darts as explained for Diagram 60.

Draw straight lines to govern the slant of the darts from H to half-way between N and O, from G to half-way between P and M, and from F to half-way between L and K.   Shape the darts as represented.   C to Q, on the sweep is 1¼ inch, and Q to R is the same.

B to S, on the sweep is 2 inches, and S to T is the same.

Draw straight lines from Q to S and from R to T.

The shaded part folds under on the line Q-S on the right side, which is the front edge of the skirt on the right side.   On the left side the fold is made on the line B C which is at the center-of-front.

The buttonholes are worked through the folded parts on one side, and the buttons are sewn through the folded parts on the other side.

The front fork part is drafted as follows: R to U is the rise, 11¼ inches from this draft.

U to V is ½ hip on the division of sixths on the ordinary tailor's square, or one-twelfth of the full hip, 3⅓ inches for this draft.

T to W is ½ inch more than from U to V.   Draw a straight line from V to W. W to X is 1½ inch.

Draw a straight line for the bottom from S to X.   U to Y is the same as U to V. Curve the fork edge as represented from Y to V.

This part—Y to V, V to X, X to T and T back to Y—passes between the legs.

The back plait, which is shaded, is drafted as follows :

I to Z is the same as B to F, 10 inches for this draft, and Z to 1 is the same.

2 is half-way between Z and 1, and 3 is half-way between I and 2.

J to 4, on the sweep is one-fourth full waist, 5¾ inches for this draft.

Draw a straight line from 2 up through 4, and square back to J by this line. This locates 5.   6 is half-way between 5 and J.   Draw the center or fold line from 6 to 3.   The back fork part is drafted as follows : 5 to 7 is ½ hip—20—on the division of sixths on the ordinary tailor's square, 3⅓ inches for this draft.   7 to 8 is the rise, 11¼ inches for this draft.   8 to 9 is the same as 2 to 1.   From 9 to 1 is

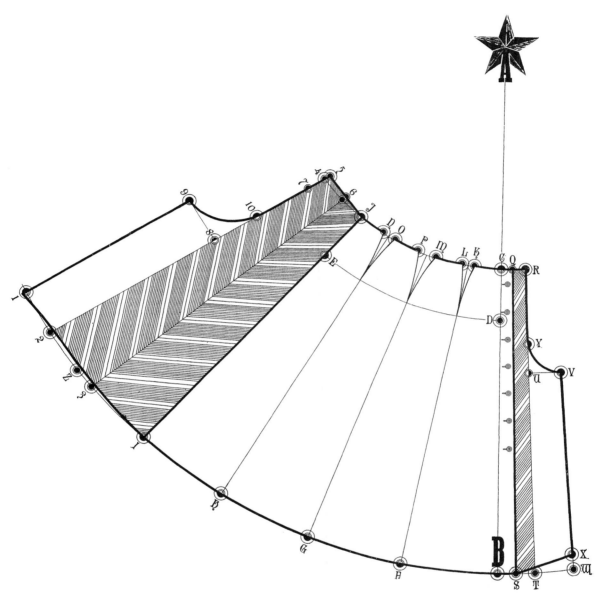

DIAGRAM 70.

the same as from V to X. Shape the bottom from 1 forward, curving it ¼ inch above Z as represented. 8 to 10 is the same as 8 to 9. Curve the fork edge as represented from 10 to 9.

This part—10 to 9, 9 to 1, 1 to 2 and 2 back to 10—passes between the legs. The edges 9 to 1 of the back fork part and V to X of the front fork part meet and are joined by a seam.

The front fork R=Y=V may be finished with a fly, as for a man, or the opening may be made below K or at the back as desired.

The waist is finished with a waistband.

VARIATIONS OF FRONT, SIDE AND BACK LENGTHS.

DIAGRAM 71.

THE front, side and back lengths will frequently vary according to the prominence of the hips or stomach, or the attitude of the client. Both of the side lengths, right and left, should be taken, as frequently one hip will be found to be higher or fuller than the other. In such cases draft both sides by the fullest side. The low or flat side should be padded.

The measures used for this diagram are as follows : 24 waist, 42 hip, 42 front length, 43½ side length, 43 back length.

The run of the waist line, in its relation to the sweep-line from C is governed by the front and side lengths only.

For this diagram Points A, B, C, F, G, I, M, 1, 2, 3, 4, 5, 6, 7, 8 and 9 are obtained in the same manner as explained for Diagram 60. After obtaining these points proceed as follows :

Pivot at C and cast short upward sweeps from 4, 5, 6, 7, 8, 9, and I.

From 7 to O, 9 to Q and I to J, are each the difference between the front and side lengths, 1½ inch for this draft.

Sweep forward from Q pivoting at the bottom of the dart to establish P, and from O to establish N.

Shape the seam from N towards C to establish L.

Sweep forward from L pivoting at the bottom of the dart to establish K.

Shape the waist-seam as represented by the solid lines.

From midway between K and L, N and O, and P and Q, draw lines for the run of the darts towards 1, 2 and 3.

Shape the darts as represented making them 5 inches deep.

Draw the center-of-back line from J, and apply the back length from J to M.

Any style of plaiting may be added back of the line J M as may be required.

DIAGRAM 72.

The measures used are as follows :

28 waist, 45 hip, and 42 front, 40½ side and 40 back length.

Points A, B, C, F, G, M, 2, 3, 4, 5, 6 and 7 are obtained in the same manner as explained for Diagram 62.

Lay a straight-edge to touch F and M, and establish I on the sweep-line from C.

Make short downward sweeps from 4, 5, 6, 7 and I, pivoting at C.

I to J, and 7 to O are each the difference between the front and side lengths, 1½ inch for this draft.

Sweep forward from O pivoting at the bottom of the dart, to establish N.

Lay a slightly curved stick touching at N and C to establish L, and sweep from L, pivoting at the bottom of the dart to establish K.

Shape the waist-seam as represented by the solid lines.

From midway between K and L, and N and O, draw straight lines to 2 and to 3, and shape the darts as represented making them 5 inches deep.

Draw the center-of-back line from J, and apply the back length from J to M.

Any style of plaiting may be added back of the line J M.

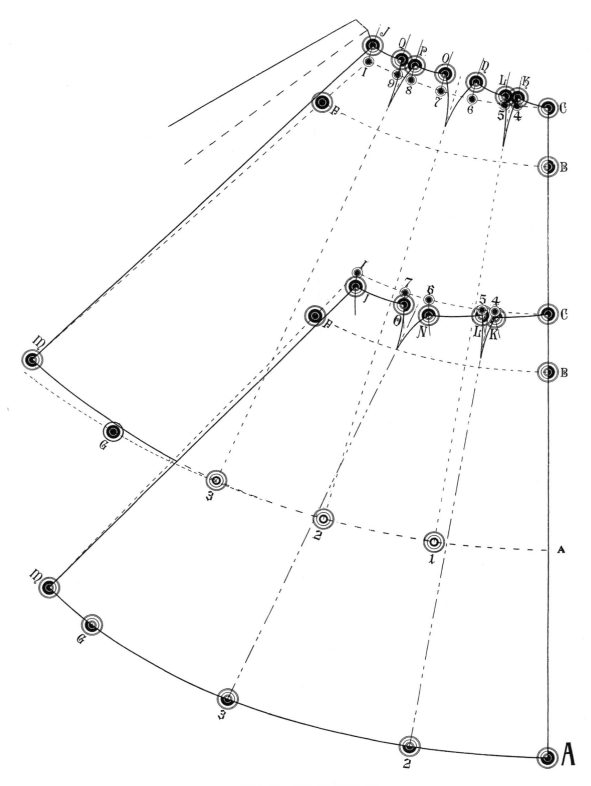

DIAGRAMS 71 AND 72.

VARIATIONS FOR PROMINENT STOMACH.

FOR forms having a prominent stomach, the front gore, if cut on the lines laid down for the preceding diagram would have an unsightly kick-out at the bottom on the crease edge.   To avoid this proceed as follows.

DIAGRAM 73.

Points A, B, C, 1, 2 and 5 define the front gore as explained for Diagram 72.

A to 3 is 2 inches.

Redraw the crease-edge from C to 3.

From 2 to 4 is the same as A to 3.

From 5 to 6 is ½ inch.

Reshape the side seam from 1 through 6 to 4, and cut out the gore as shown by the shaded part.

The same amount must be taken from the front edge of the side gore as has been added to the front gore from 2 to 4.

DIAGRAM 74.

The changed front gore shown by the shaded part on Diagram 73 is shown by the broken lines on this diagram and defined by the corresponding points C, 3, 4, 6 and 2. The material having first been cut out on these lines (C to 3 being laid on the fold), a strong round must be forced by the iron on the fold edge of the material as at 8, and the round on the side at 6 correspondingly worked forward as to 7.

The requisite front length, in its proper relation to the side length, together with the changes above described and the shaping given by the iron to the front gore will cause the center-of-front line to hang below the prominence of the abdomen, straight to the bottom.

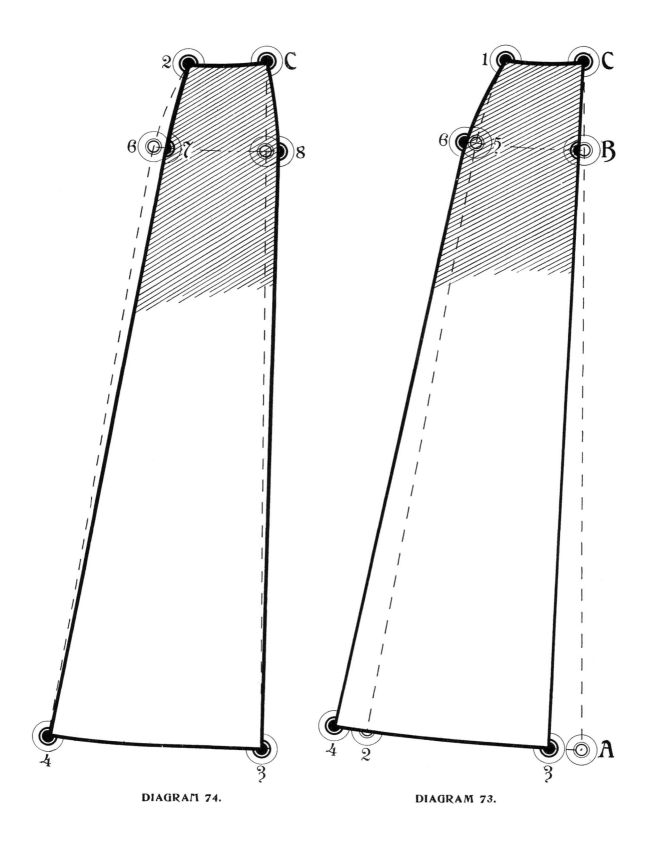

DIAGRAM 74.   DIAGRAM 73.

CROSS SADDLE RIDING SKIRT.

DIAGRAM 75.

THE measures used for the accompanying diagram are as follows : 24 waist, 42 hip, 40 front, side and back lengths, 12 hip rise.

TO DRAFT.

Draw a straight line as A D. A to B is the front length. B to C is 5½ inches. B to D is the full waist, 24 inches. Pivot at D and sweep from B, C and A. C to E is one-half of the full hip.

A to 1, 1 to 2, 2 to 3, 3 to F and F to 4 are each ½ hip, 10½ inches.

Draw a straight line from 4 through E to establish G.

By measuring along the waist line from B to G we find that we have for this draft 16 inches, which is 4 inches more than one-half of the full waist. This surplus is disposed of as follows: B to 5 is ¼ waist, or ⅛ of the full waist, 3 inches for this draft. From 5 to 6 is one-fourth of the waist surplus, 1 inch for this draft. From 6 to 7 is the same as B to 5. G to 8 is the same as B to 5. From 8 to 9 is the same as from 5 to 6. From 9 to 10 is the same as B to 5.

From midway between 5 and 6, 7 and 10, and 8 and 9 draw a straight line towards 1, 2 and 3 respectively, and shape the darts as represented.

B to H is 2½ inches, and 11 is half-way between B and H.

A to I is 5 inches, and 12 is half-way beween A and I.

Connect 11 and 12. Connect H and I.

H to J is the hip rise. J to K, J to 14 and I to 13 are each ⅙ hip, 3½ inches for this draft. Connect K and 13.

From 13 to 15 is 1½ inch. Shape the bottom from 12 to 15 and the fork K to 14 as represented.

The line A B is at the center-of-front. The top or right side folds under on the line 1 to 12. This brings the line H I directly under the line B A. The under or left side folds under on the center-of-front line A B. It is then folded forwards on the line 11 to 12. This brings the line H I directly under the center-of-front line A B. Buttons are sewn on the left side, and buttonholes are worked on the right side as represented. When dismounted the fronts are closed by the button-holes and buttons.

The fronts from H to K may be closed with a fly and buttons, or the opening may be made at the sides below 5, or at the back as desired.

From 4 to L is 1½ inch. Connect G and L. L to M is any desired width for a plait. On the diagram L to M is 6 inches. M to N is 1½ inch.

G to Q is 2½ inches. Connect M and Q. Connect N and Q. N to O is 1½ inch more than L to N. Q to R is the same as G to Q. Connect R and O.

Run a tracing-wheel along the lines G L and Q N.

Fold all of the paper which is back of the line G L underneath, first on the line Q N, then on the line G L. Open out the folds and bring the fold G L directly over the line Q M. This gives the underfold line 16 to 17.

Fold the crease-line Q N back directly over the line R O. This gives the underfold line 18 to 19.

When the plaits are folded in this manner, all of the shaded parts will lie underneath and forward of the line G L. When they are thus folded cut across the top on the line 8 to G. R is now directly under G. R to S is ⅙ hip, 3½ inches for this draft. S to U is the hip rise.

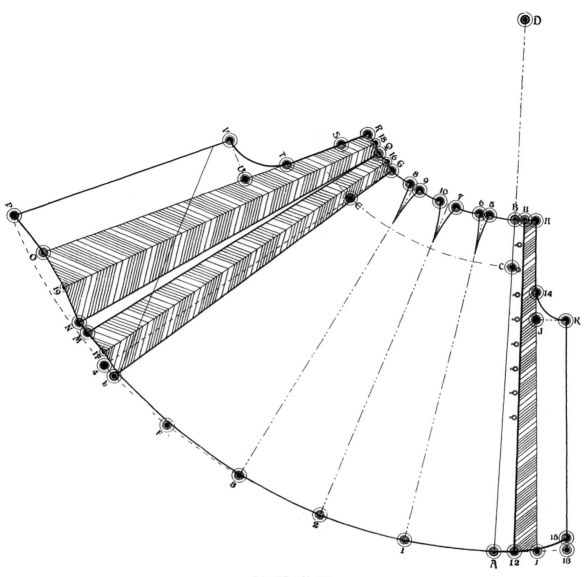

DIAGRAM 75.

U to T, U to V and O towards P are each ¼ hip, 5¼ inches for this draft.

Apply the back length from G towards L.

V to P is the same as K to 15.

With the plaits folded as above explained, M and O will lie directly under L, the shaded parts forward of the line G L, and the unshaded parts back of the line G L. Now cut from P across the plaits towards the back length near L and from there to the side length at 2. Upon unfolding the plaits the run of the top from G to R, and of the bottom from P to 2 will be as defined by the solid lines.

K 15 joins V P.

The pattern should be laid with the line from 2 to the second dart directly over the opened crease or fold of the material. For this size and with goods 56 inches wide, a wheel-piece would be required at the back only, as shown by the light line extending from just below V to L.

EQUESTRIAN SKIRT.

(SIDE-SADDLE.)

DIAGRAM 76.

THE measures used are as follows :
24 waist, 42 hip, 39 side-length, 17 front of waist to point of knee when seated on dummy horse.

TO DRAFT THE FRONT.

Square the lines A E and A T.

A to B is the side-length, 39 inches. B to C is ¾ inch more than ⅙ hip, 4¼ inches. B to D is ⅓ of the full side length, 13 inches. B to E is 1 inch more than ⅓ waist, 5 inches.

Square across from C and E, and sweep forward from B, pivoting at D.

E to F is ⅔ waist, 8 inches.

A to G is one-half of the full hip, 21 inches. G to H is ⅛ hip, 2⅝ inches. Draw a straight line from H through F.

F to I is ⅛ waist, 1½ inch. I to J is ⅙ waist, 2 inches. J to K is ½ waist, 6 inches.

Pivot at I and sweep forward from K towards L, and backward towards O.

K to L is ⅓ waist, 4 inches. Pivot at J and sweep from L to establish M.

M to N is ⅙ waist, 2 inches. K to O is 1 inch more than ½ waist, 7 inches. Shape from O to D, and from O through K to L as represented.

C to Q is the full hip, 42 inches. Q to R is 1 inch less than ¼ hip, 4¼ inches.

A to S is the full hip, 42 inches. S to T is 6 inches. Square up from T. T to U is 3 inches. Connect R and U.

R to V is ⅓ of the length, R to U. V to W is 1½ inch. Shape the seam from R through W to U, and the bottom from A through G to U as represented.

L to X is 1 inch more than the knee length, 18 inches. Pivot at L and sweep down from X.

X to Y is ⅙ hip, 3½ inches.

Pivot at Y and sweep back from R towards Z.

R to Z is 1½ inch more than ¼ hip, 6¾ inches. Shape the dart from Y to R, and Y to Z as represented.

Connect M and Z by a straight line. Half-way between M and Z establish 1. From 1 to 2 is 1¼ inch. Shape the seam from M through 2 to Z as represented.

Half-way between L and N establish 3. Connect 3 and Y.

Y to 5 is 3 inches.

Shape the dart from L and N to 5 as represented. O to 6 is 2 inches.

A O is the left side and seams to A I of the back.

The line H K is the center of front. The opening is at 6. It is 9 inches deep, and is closed with a fly. A pocket may be inserted in the opening at 6 if desired.

For a proportionate pattern when the knee-length is not obtainable, from L to X may be made 2½ inches less than half of the full hip.

A heel strap is fitted at the lower front as illustrated.

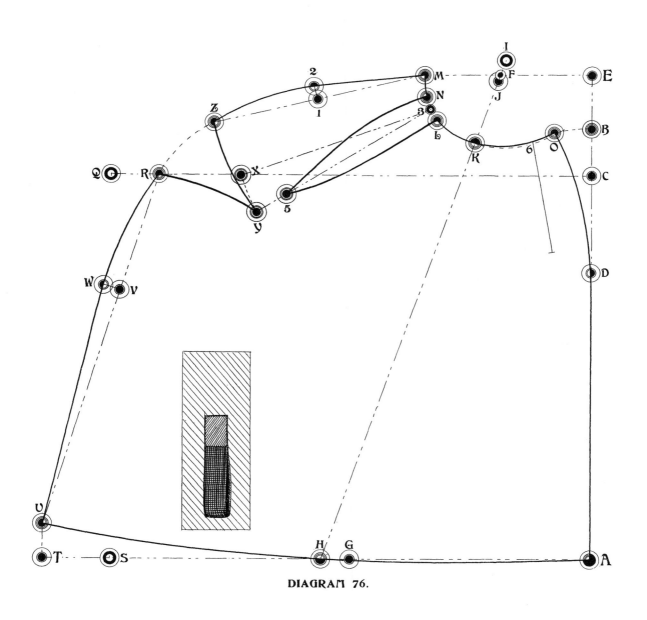

DIAGRAM 76.

Equestrian Skirt.

(SIDE SADDLE.)

(*Concluded.*)

DIAGRAM 77.

TO DRAFT THE BACK.

Square the lines A F and A Y.

A to B is the side-length, 39 inches.

B to C is ¾ inch more than ⅙ hip, 4¼ inches.   B to D is ⅔ waist, 8 inches. B to E is one-half of the full waist, 12 inches.   E to F is ½ waist, 6 inches.   Square out from C and D.

B to 1 is one-third of the full side-length, 13 inches.   Sweep back from B, pivoting at 1.   B to I is one-half of B to O on the front.

D to G is half of the full waist, 12 inches.   G to H is ¼ waist, 3 inches.

Pivot at F and sweep from H towards I.

H to J is 1 inch more than ½ waist, 7 inches.   Measure on the waist line of the front from O to L and N to M.   Place this at H on the back and measure to I, following the sweep line.   For this draft, the waist as thus defined measures 29¾ inches, which is 5¾ inches more than the waist size required.   This 5¾ inches is taken out by the dart as follows: Place one-half of it from J to V, and one-half from J to W.

H to L is the same as M to Z on the front.   Shape the seam from H to L, and the side-seam from I through 1 as represented.

Draw a straight line from F through J.

J to U is 1½ inch more than ½ hip, 12 inches.

Cast a short upward sweep from V, pivoting at I, also from W, pivoting at H. V to 2 is ⅜ inch.   Pivot at U and sweep back from 2 to establish 3.   Shape the dart as represented.   Connect D and L, and by this line square down from L.

L to M is 2 inches more than ⅓ hip, 9 inches.   Pivot at M and sweep from L towards N.

L to N is ¾ inch more than ¼ hip, 6 inches.   Draw a line from M through N.

N to O is 2 inches.   P is half-way from L to N.   Pivot at P and sweep from M towards R.

O to T is half-way from O to M.   T to Q is 1 inch and Q to S is the same. Draw a line from L through Q to establish R.

Pivot at R and sweep forward and backward from Q.   Shape the pommel cut (L M S R T O) as represented by the solid lines.

A to Y is 3 inches less than the full hip, 39 inches.   Connect O and Y.

O to Z is one-third of the full length, O to Y.   Square out at Z.

Z to 4 is 1½ inch.   Shape the seam from O through 4 and Y, and make the length from O to X the same as R to U on the front.

Shape the bottom A to X as represented.

A 1 is the left side.   The seat is at U.   A tab is sewed on the underside of the jacket below the natural waist line, in which two buttonholes are worked, the eyes of which are opposite the back-tack.   Two buttons are sewed on the skirt as represented near V, which secure the skirt to the buttonholes in the tab.   A small loop is attached to the skirt below M, which must be adjusted when the lady is standing. When dismounted this loop is slipped over a third button, about 2 inches below the tab button at the right.

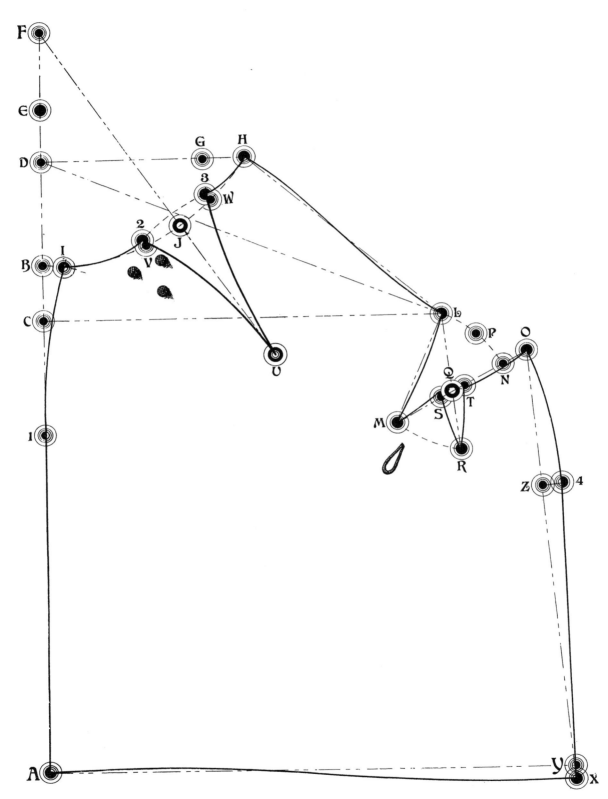

DIAGRAM 77.

TROUSERS.

DIAGRAM 78.

THE measures used for this diagram are as follows :
10½ hip rise, 42 side length, 43½ front length, 24 waist, 40 seat, 17½ knee, 15 bottom.

The hip rise is obtained by measuring from the top of the hip at the side to the top of the chair seat when the lady is seated.

The side length is taken from the same point at the top of the hip to the heel seam of the shoe.

The front length is taken from the center-of-front at the waist to the heel-seam at side of foot.

The waist is taken close.

The seat is taken close over the fullest part.

The knee size can be estimated.

The bottom is taken according to style.

All seams are included on this draft.

To Draft the Forepart.

Square the lines A J and A D.

A to B is the hip rise. A to D is the side length. B to C is 1 inch less than half-way from B to D. Square the cross-lines from B, C and D.

B to H is ⅔ seat, 13⅜ inches for this draft. F is half-way from B to H. G is half-way from F to H. Square up from G and F to establish J and K.

G to M is ⅙ seat. Draw a line from H to M. N is half-way from H to M. Connect G and N. N to O is ¾ inch.

D to E is ⅙ seat. Connect E and F to establish P.

P to Q is ¼ knee, and P to R is the same.

Deduct 3 inches from the size at the bottom, and place ¼ of the remainder, from E to 1, and the same amount from E to S. For this draft E to 1 and E to S are each 3 inches.

Cast a sweep for the front length as at I, pivoting at 1.

K to the sweep line at I is ¼ waist.

I to L is ½ and ⅛ waist, 7½ inches for this draft. The above ⅛ waist is taken out by the dart distributed equally on each side of K. This establishes 2 and 3.

Shape the front from I through M and O to H as represented. Shape the side-seam from L through B and Q to 1, and the inseam from H through R to S.

Shape the bottom from 1 to S rounding 1 inch above E.

Cut out the pattern making notches at B, Q and R.

To Draft the Back.

Lay the pattern of the forepart over another piece of paper and proceed as follows :

Sweep from a point ¼ inch above L towards V, and from B towards 7, pivoting at Q. Extend the crosslines at the knee and bottom.

T is half-way from G to J. Connect B and T.

Square up from T, by the line B T, towards U. On the line just drawn establish U ¼ seat above the line A J.

U to 4 is ½ waist. From 4 to 5 is ⅛ waist. From 5 to V is 2 inches always. Square back from T to establish 6. From 6 to W is 3 inches always. R to Y is 1 inch always. Pivot midway between R and Y and cast a short sweep back from H.

H to Z is 1/12 seat.

Shape the back-seam from U through T and N to Z as represented.

E to X is 1 inch.

S to E and X to 8 is ½ inch more than half of the full size of the bottom.

X to 9 is the same as X to 8.

Shape the side-seam from V through W and Q to 9, and the inseam from Z through Y to 8 as represented.

Shape the bottom from 8 to 9 rounding ½ inch below X.

Cut out the pattern making notches at 7, Q and Y.

The opening may be made at the sides or at the front, and is closed with a fly. The tops are finished with a regular waistband cut 2 inches wide.

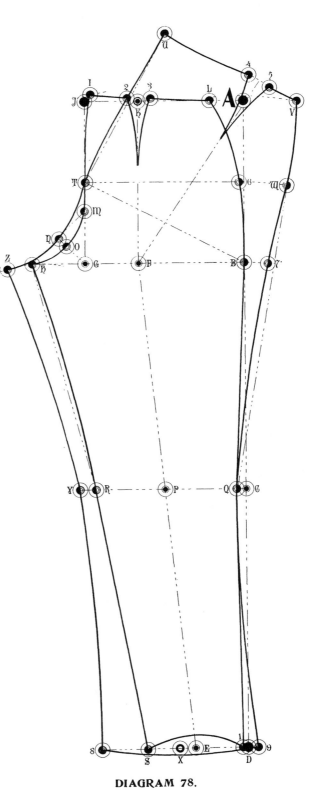

DIAGRAM 78.

RIDING BREECHES.

DIAGRAM 79.

THE measures used for the accompanying diagram are as follows: 11 hip rise, 24 length to knee, 28 to calf, 38 to ankle, 42 side length as for trousers, 43½ front length as for trousers, 24 waist, 40 seat, 14½ knee, 14½ calf, 8½ ankle.

To Draft the Forepart.

Square the lines A J and A F.

A to B is the hip rise. A to C is 2 inches more than the length to knee. A to D is 2 inches more than the length to calf. A to E is 2 inches more than the length to ankle. A to F is 2 inches more than the side length.

Z is half-way from A to B. Square the cross lines from Z, B, C, D, E and F.

B to I is ⅔ seat. G is half-way from B to I. H is half-way from G to I. Square up from H and G to establish J and K.

H to M is ⅙ seat. Connect I and M. N is half-way from I to M. Connect N and H. N to O is ¾ inch.

F to 17 is ⅙ seat. Connect 17 and G. This establishes P, Q and 1.

Apply 2 inches more than the front length from F by a sweep as to X. K to X is ¼ waist. Shape the front from X through M and O to I as represented.

X to L is ½ and ⅛ waist. H to 2 and H to 3 are each 1/16 waist. Shape the side-seam from L to B as represented. From 1 to V and 1 to W are each ¼ ankle. P to R and P to S are each ¼ knee. Q to T and Q to U are each ¼ calf.

Draw guide-lines from I to R, and B to S. Shape the side-seam below B through S and U to W, and the in-seam from I through R and T to V as represented. Shape the waist-seam from L to X, and the V below 2 and 3, making the V 4½ inches deep.

To Draft the Backpart.

Cut out the pattern of the forepart, making notches at B, R and S, and lay it over another piece of paper. Extend the cross-lines at C, D and E.

Sweep from a point ¼ inch above L towards 6, pivoting at S, also from I towards 9, pivoting ½ inch back of R. H to Y is half of the hip rise. Connect B and Y.

Square up by the line B Y towards 16, and on this line establish 16, ¼ of the seat above the line A J where it crosses the line Y to 16.

From 16 to 4 is ½ waist. From 4 to 5 is ⅛ waist. From 5 to 6 is 2 inches always. Z to 7 is 3 inches. I to 9 is 1/12 seat. R to 11 is 1 inch. T to 12 is 1 inch. 1 to 14 is 1 inch. 1 to 13 is 2 inches. The shaded part represents a V which is to be cut out from the back, and 14 is at the center of the back.

V to 15 is ¾ inch more than ¼ ankle, and 1 to 10 is the same. Outline between all the points as represented by the solid lines and cut out the pattern making notches at 8, S, U, 11 and 12.

The opening may be made at the sides from L to B, although it is frequently made at the front below to X and closed with a fly. The tops are finished with a regular band. The side-seams are vented from the knee to the bottom.

All seams are included on this draft.

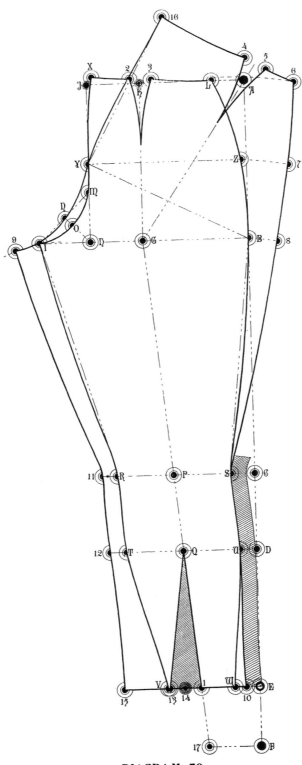

DIAGRAM 79.

KNEE=BREECHES.

DIAGRAM 80.

THE measures used are as follows: 12 hip rise, 24 length to knee, 26 to small of knee, 30 side length, 42 side length as for trousers, 44 front length, 26 waist, 44 seat, 15 knee, 13½ small of knee, 14½ bottom.

To Draft the Forepart.

Square the lines A J and A E.

A to B is the hip-rise. A to C is 1 inch more than the length to knee. A to D is 1 inch more than the length to the small of knee, and A to E is 1 inch more than the side length.

Square the cross lines from B, C, D and E.

All of the upper part on and above the fork line, is drafted in the same manner as already explained for the two preceding diagrams. To draft the lower part, proceed as follows:

Square down from F to establish P.

P to I is 1½ inch.

Draw a line from F through I to establish Q and Z.

I to R and I to S are each ¼ of the full size at the knee.

Q to T and Q to U are each ¼ of the full size at the small of knee.

Z to V and Z to W are each ¼ of the full size of the bottom.

Outline the side-seam from B through S and U to W, and the inseam from H through R and T to V.

Shape the bottom from W to V rounding ½ inch below Z.

Cut out the pattern, making notches at B, S and R.

To Draft the Backpart.

All of that part which is on and above the fork line is drafted in the same manner as explained for the two preceding diagrams. To draft the lower part proceed as follows:

R to 10, T to 11, and V to 12 are each 1 inch.

Shape the inseam from 9 through 10 and 11 to 12 as represented.

Shape the side-seam from 6 through 7, S and U to W, and cut out the pattern, making notches at 8, 10 and S.

The side-seam is vented below S, and the vent is closed with a fly and buttons. The tops are finished with a regular waistband. The opening may be made at the sides, though frequently the breeches are made fly front.

All seams are included on this draft.

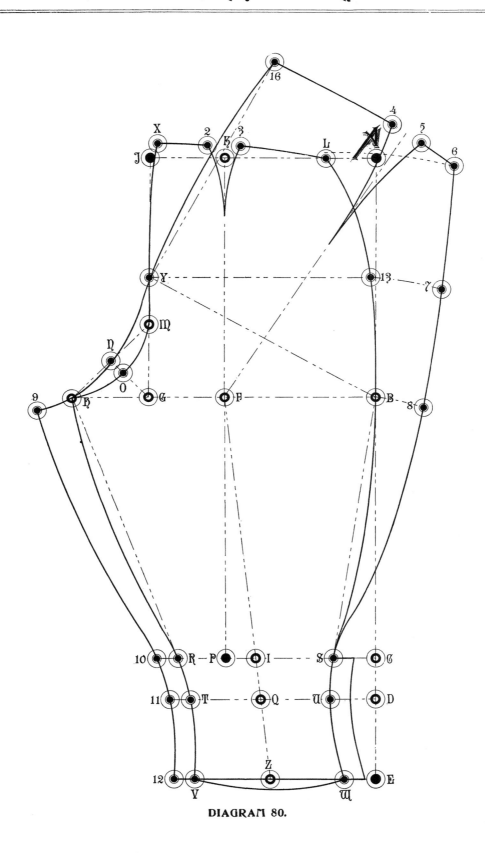

DIAGRAM 80.

KNICKERBOCKERS.

DIAGRAM 81.

THE measures used for the accompanying diagram are as follows: 11 hip-rise, 23 length to bottom of knee, 40 side length as for trousers, 42 front length as for trousers, 24 waist, 40 seat, 14 size below knee.

To Draft the Forepart.

Square the lines A J and A E. A to B is the hip-rise. A to C is the length to the bottom of knee. C to D is from 2 to 3 inches as desired for the fall. D to E is the same as C to D. Square the cross-lines from B, C, D and E.

All that part of the front which is on and above the line B H is drafted in the same manner as explained for the preceding diagrams, except that the outside-seam is shaped from L through a point ½ inch back of B. After having drafted the upper part, proceed as follows:

Square down from F to establish P and Z.

Z to S and Z to T are each ¼ of the full size below the knee.

Shape the side-seam from B to any desired degree of fullness at the knee, as through R to T.

Shape the inseam from H to S, making the width from P to Q the same as P to R.

The dart at the bottom is 1 inch wide, distributed equally on each side of Z, as from U to V. Shape the bottom from S to T, passing ½ inch below Z as represented. Cut out the pattern, making notches at B, Q and R.

To Draft the Backpart.

Lay the pattern of the forepart over another piece of paper.

Extend the cross-lines at the knee and bottom.

Sweep from H towards 9, pivoting at Q. H to 9 is $\frac{1}{12}$ seat.

Sweep from a point ¼ inch above L towards 6, pivoting at R, also from B towards 8.

All of the remainder of the back above the line 8 to 9 is drafted in the same manner as explained for the preceding diagrams. To draft the part below, proceed as follows: Q to 10, R to 11 and T to 14 are each ½ inch.

Shape the side-seam from 6 through 7 and 11 to 14.

S to U, V to T, and 14 to 12 is 1½ inch more than the size at the bottom of knee. Shape the inseam from 9 through 10 to 12 as represented.

The bottom is shaped straight across from 12 to 14.

The side-seam is vented below the fall, and closed with a fly. The top is finished with a regular band cut 2 inches wide, and the bottom with a band 1 inch wide. Make notches at 8, 10 and 11. The opening is at the side.

All seams have been allowed for on this draft.

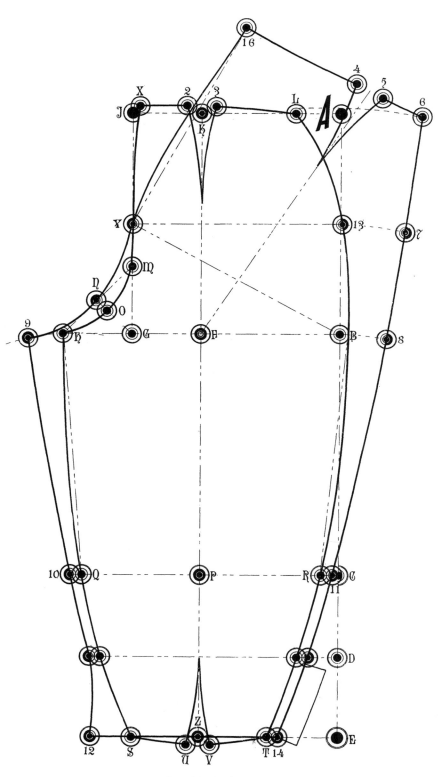

DIAGRAM 81.

BLOOMERS.

DIAGRAM 82.

THE measures required are the rise, from waist to the top of the chair seat when the lady is seated, the length from the waist to the bottom of the knee, the waist *close*, the seat, taken medium close over the skirt, and the size just below the the knee taken *close*.

The measures used are as follows:

11 rise, 23 length, 24 waist, 42 seat, 12½ below the knee.

TO DRAFT.

Square the lines A E and A K.

A to B is the rise, 11 inches.

A to C is the length, 23 inches.

As the bloomers are to be baggy below the knee, extra length must be added. If it is desired that they shall fall 4 inches below the knee, twice that quantity must be added, as from C to D. E is turned up on the underside to C and is held in place by the band at the bottom.

Square the cross-lines from B, C and D.

B to F is ½ seat, 10½ inches.

F to G is $\frac{1}{12}$ seat, 1¾ inch.

G to J is ⅓ seat, 7 inches.

H is half-way between G and J.

Square up from G. This establishes K. Square down from J. This establishes O.

O to P is 2½ inches, and D to E is 1 inch.

Connect J and P, and P and E as represented.

K to L is 1 inch. Connect A and L.

Draw a straight line from H through L.

L to M is ⅙ seat, 3½ inches.

H to N is 2 inches.

Shape from M through L and N to J, and from M to A as represented.

The forepart is defined by points A, L, J, P, E and A, and the backpart by A, M, J, P, E and A.

Cut the band for the bottom ½ inch more than the full size below the knee. The waistband is cut one-half of the full waist with an overlap of 1½ inch added. It is 2½ inches wide. The opening is at the side, and is closed with buttons. A pocket may be put in at the opening if desired.

The bottom is gathered to the band and the side-seam is left open about 7 inches above the band. The opening is closed with buttons.

The waist is gathered on to the waistband, or laid in plaits as may be preferred. No linings are used except for the waistband. Strips of the material are sewn to the center-of-front and at the sides and back, through which the belt is to be drawn.

All seams are allowed on this draft.

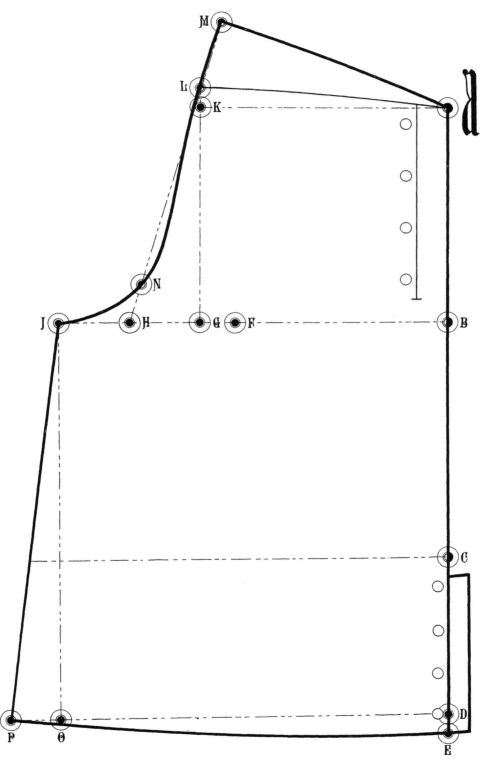

DIAGRAM 82.

LEGGINGS.

DIAGRAM 83.

THE measures used for the accompanying diagram are as follows: 4½ from floor to ankle, 13½ floor to calf, 17 floor to top, 12½ size at top, 14½ calf, 9 ankle, 13 instep, 17¼ bottom.

TO DRAFT.

Draw a line as A E.
A to C is the height to ankle.
A to D is the height to calf.
A to E is the height to top.
B is half-way from A to C.
A to N is 1 inch.
Square the cross-lines from B, C, D, E and N.
E to G is half of the full size at the top.
D to H is half of the full size at the calf.
C to I is ½ inch.
I to J is half of the full size of ankle.
I to K is half of the full instep.
K to M is half of the full bottom.
Outline as shown by the solid lines.
The button line is half-way between E and G, and C and J. The line F L is ½ inch back of the button line. Add a button stand to the underside as represented by the broken line from 1 to 2.

The inside is cut in one piece, and is defined by points E, G, K, M and E. The outside is cut in two pieces, the front being defined by points E, F, L, M and E, and the back by G, K, 1, 2 and G.

Add for all seams when cutting the material.

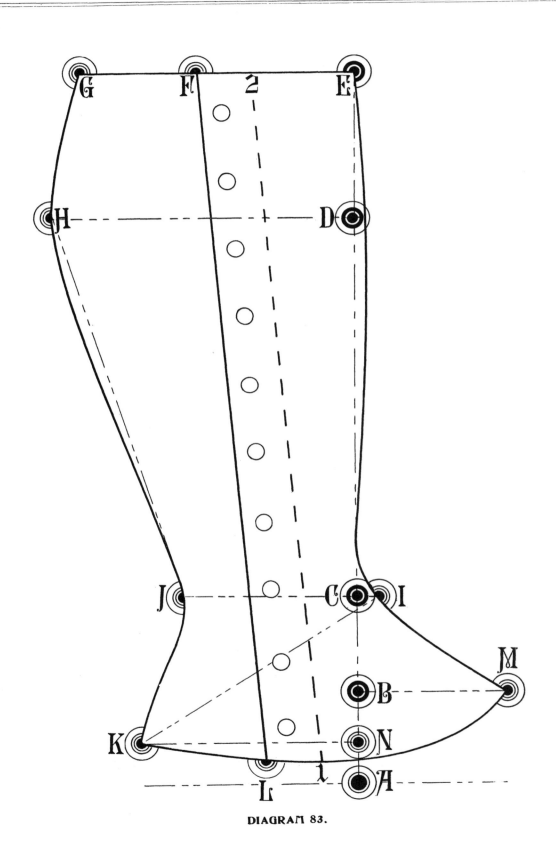

DIAGRAM 83.

THE RAGLAN BOX COAT.

DIAGRAM 84.

THE measures used are as follows :

7 back-scye depth, 15½ length to natural waist, 38 length, 10 blade, 11¼ front-scye depth, 15½ over-shoulder, 9 front-hip, 36 bust, 42 hip.

TO DRAFT.

Points A, C, C1, D, E, F, G, H, L, M, N, O, Q, W, 8, 11, 12, 13, 18 and 25 are obtained in the same manner as explained for Diagram 15.

Square backward from D.

Draw a straight line from E through C1.   This establishes X.

Connect A and X.

Half-way between 18 and the front of scye establish B.

Square down from B to establish R.

R to J is ½ inch. R to K is 1½ inch.

Draw a straight line from B through J.   This establishes S.

Draw a straight from B through K.   This establishes T.

Pivot at M and sweep forward from the length directly below M to establish V.

B to U is the same as B to V.

Pivot at 12 and sweep a short distance forward and backward from W. Shape the bottom from U to W as represented.

From the bust-line to 2 is one-fourth of the full scye.

From 2 to 3 is ⅜ inch.

N to 17 is ½ or ¾ inch.

Shape the raglan shoulder from 17 through 3 and from L to the back-scye as represented.

The pattern should be cut as for a square shoulder from L to 8 and N to 11. When the raglan sleeve has been drafted, the square shoulder may then be cut off or not below L and 17 as desired.

Q to Z is the front hip.

The construction of this diagram gives ample fullness around the hips, as will be seen by measuring on the hip-line from Z to T and S to the center-of-back opposite C1.   For this draft the size around the hip is 48 inches, or 6 inches more than the hip measure.   It may be diminished by lessening the quantity between J and K It may be increased by establishing point 3 and proceeding as explained for Diagram 90.

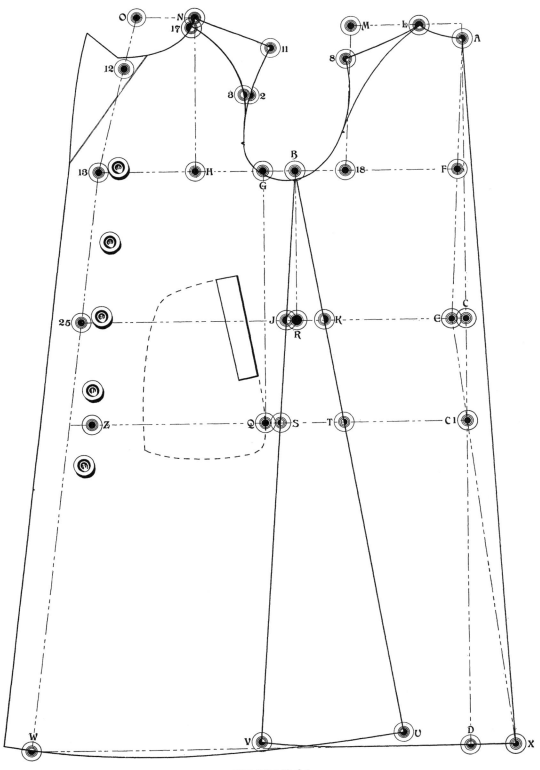

DIAGRAM 84.

THE RAGLAN SLEEVE.

DIAGRAM 85.

THE measures used are as follows: 16½ scye, 9 underarm-scye, 8 length to elbow, 17½ length, 9 cuff, 11½ elbow.

The first and second measures are obtained by measuring the pattern of the coat after it has been drafted in the same manner as explained for Diagram 23.

TO DRAFT.

Fold a piece of paper lengthwise, thus forming a crease-line. Open out the fold and lay the paper with the hollow of the crease underneath. The heavy line from star to star represents the crease-line.

Establish B on the crease-line. B to the lower star is 24 inches always. From the star to 1 is 1 inch. Draw a straight line from 1 up through B towards A.

B to C is the same as from the notch to the bust line at front of scye. C to A is ¼ of the full scye. Square back from A and C by the line A1, and extend the line from C forward across the paper. A to F is ¼ of the full scye, and F to G is the same. Square up from F. G to H is $\frac{1}{12}$ of the full scye.

C to D is the length to elbow. C to E is the length. D to O is 1½ inch. Square from O by E towards J. O to J is one-half the size at elbow.

Cast a sweep from E towards M, pivoting at G. E to M is half the size at the cuff. Place the pattern of the forepart over the sleeve draft with the bust line directly over the line which is squared each way from C, and the front scye notch touching the crease-line as at B. Mark along the edge of the forepart from 3 to B and up just past A, as shown by the broken line. Place the back touching the forepart as at 3, keeping the bust line directly over the line which is squared each way from C. Mark along the edge of the back-scye as shown by the broken line. Make a cross mark and notch the back where it is desired that the back-arm-seam shall join the back of the coat, as at R.

Shape the under-sleeve-head from B, passing ¼ inch above 3 as represented by the solid line. Apply the underarm-scye measure from B, following the solid line just past 3, and from there swing the tape until the measure (which for this draft is 9 inches), strikes the line A G. For this draft this measure reaches H. Finish the run of the under-sleeve-head in the direction of H as represented.

From B, following the solid line to 6 is ¼ inch more than from B, following the broken line to the notch at R. Shape the seam from 6 through J to M as represented. Pivot at J and sweep back from 6. Connect H and J. This establishes 10. From 10 to 9 is the same as from 6 to 10. Shape the seam from 9 through J as represented. B to I, in a straight line, is 1½ inch more than from B following the shape of the raglan shoulder seam to 17. Lay the pattern of the forepart with the front shoulder point N at I, and the square-shoulder seam touching the line I F. The position of the forepart is shown in light circled lines.

With a tracing-wheel mark the shape of the raglan shoulder seam from 17. This establishes P. Remove the pattern of the forepart. P to S is 1 inch less than from N to 11. Shape the seam from P through S to B as shown by the broken line.

Now lay the pattern of the back with L at I and the square shoulder-seam touching the line I F. The position of the back is shown in light circled lines.

With a tracing-wheel mark the shape of the raglan shoulder-seam from L or I. Remove the pattern. I to T is the same as P to S. Shape the seam from I through T and H to 9 as represented by the broken line.

The lines 9, H, T, I, P, S, B, define the top of the raglan top-sleeve without the dart. They are sometimes made with the dart to gain extra length and ease over the outer shoulder. In such case proceed as follows:

From a point half-way between I and P, square down to establish Q.

Sweep forward and backward from P, pivoting at Q. P to U and I to V are each $\frac{1}{16}$ of the full scye.

Lay a piece of paper underneath the draft and run a tracing-wheel on the line A G, and above the line A G from H through T, I, P and S as far as the line A G.

Cut out the piece just defined and place it over the draft on the line A G. Hold it at the front edge on the line A G and swing the top forward until it touches U.

Mark along the edge and across the top at W, and connect W and Q as represented.

Now hold the piece with the back edge at H on the line A G. Pivot at H and swing the top backward until it touches V. Mark along the edge and across the top at X, and connect X and Q as represented.

Fold the pattern on the first crease-line from star to star and cut through both thicknesses of paper from E to M, and M through J to 9, X, Q, W and B. If the dart is not desired cut above 9 through H, T, I, P, S to B. Open out the fold and cut singly from J to 6 and B. The pattern will then appear as shown on Diagram 24, excepting the oval-shaped top-sleeve-head. Establish the forearm-seam in the manner explained for Diagram 25. Make a notch at B.

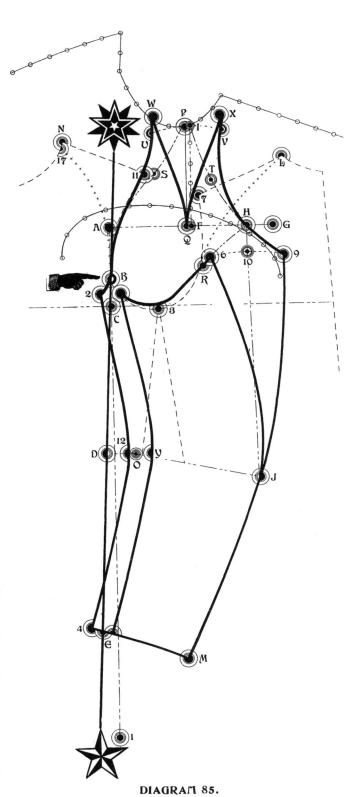

DIAGRAM 85.

PLAIN ULSTER.

DIAGRAM 86.

SQUARE the lines 1 K and 1 D.

From 1 to A is $\frac{1}{24}$ bust. A to B is the back-scye depth. A to C is the natural waist length. A to D is the length. C to C1 is 5½ inches. Square the cross-lines from B, C, C1 and D.

C to E is $\frac{1}{12}$ bust for all sizes of 36 bust and under. For sizes above 36 bust C to E is 1½ inch. Connect A and E. This establishes F. E to 2 is to taste or style. For this diagram E to 2 is 1¾ inch. Square down from E and 2 to establish 3 and 4. From 3 to N1 is 2 inches, and 4 to Q1 is the same. Shape the back skirt as represented.

T to U is the back-waist. U to E represents the back-waist surplus. Complete the back and shoulder sections in the same manner as explained for diagram 5.

Obtain all the points through the back-waist in the same manner as explained for diagram 6.

Square down from 13 to establish P. P to 24 is 1 inch. Draw a straight line from 13 through 24 to establish 30 and 32. Half-way between G and 13 establish 25. For this diagram, point 23 is half-way between T and 24. Draw a straight line from 25 through 23 to establish 28 and 33.

U to V is one-half of the full waist. V to 24 represents the front-waist surplus. The fronts are half-tight fitting. One-half of the front-waist surplus is therefore taken out by the dart, which is distributed equally on each side of 23. This establishes 21 and 22. From 25 to 31 is one-third of the distance from 25 to 23.

Q to Z is 1 inch less than the front-hip. Z to 32 represents the front-hip surplus, one half of which is taken out by the dart distributed equally on each side of 28. Shape the dart as represented.

G to 19 is ½ inch less than T to 17. Draw a straight line from 19 through 17 to establish W and 29. From 19 to 20 is ¼ inch less than half-way from 19 to the side-seam of the back. Draw a straight line through 20 and 15 to establish X.

The hip spring at W and X is obtained in the same manner as explained for diagram 6.

To obtain the run of the lines below the hip-line, proceed as follows: Extend the line which is drawn from 8 through 14 down to the bottom of the draft, and, using this as a guide line, shape the back edge of the sidebody below Y to P1 as represented.

Shape the back edge of the underarmpiece from the hip-line towards O1 *parallel* with the line from Y to P1.

Shape the side-seam of the forepart below the hip-line towards M1 *parallel* with the back edge of the underarmpiece.

Shape the front edge of the underarmpiece below the hip-line towards K1 *parallel* with the guide line through W to 29.

Shape the front edge of the sidebody below the hip-line towards L1 *parallel* with the front edge of the underarmpiece.

Obtain the sweeping points on the bust-line and shape the bottom as explained for diagram 6.

The center-of-front is defined by points 12, 13, 24 and 30. Any amount may be added forward of this line according to the current style.

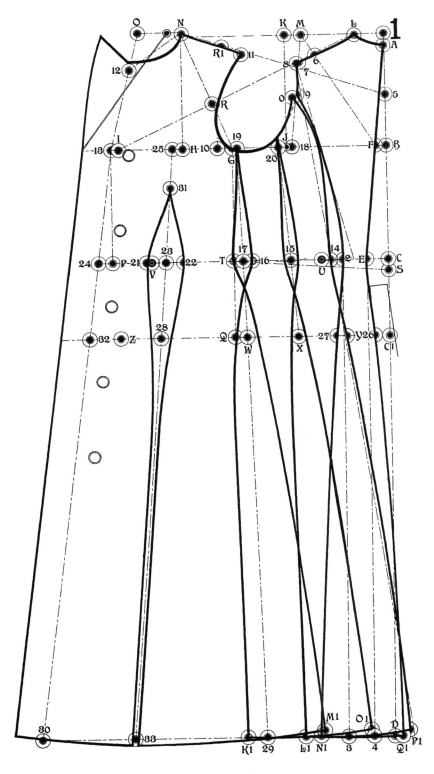

DIAGRAM 86.

THREE=SEAM COAT.

DIAGRAM 87.

THIS garment is drafted to fit fair around the hips. It is half-shapely at the back-waist and has a box-front. It is drafted from the following measures: 6 half-width of back, 7 back-scye depth, 15¼ length to natural waist, 38 length, 10 blade, 11¼ front-scye depth, 15¼ over-shoulder, 6¼ back-waist, 9 front-hip, 36 bust, 25 waist, 42 hip.

TO DRAFT.

A to B is the back-scye depth. A to C is the length to natural waist. A to D is the length. C to C1 is 5½ inches. Square the cross-lines.

C to E is ¾ inch. Connect A and E to establish F.

Points G, T, P, Q, Z, 12 and 13 and all that part which is above the bust line, excepting the lapel are obtained in the same manner as explained for the preceding diagram. P to M is 1 inch.

Draw a straight line from 13 through M to establish Y.

E to I is ⅙ bust. Square down from E and I to establish 1 and 2.

From 1 to 9 and from 2 to J are each ½ inch. Draw guide lines from E through 9 and from I through J.

Shape the center-back seam below E through 9 towards U as represented.

F to H is ¼ bust. H to L is ½ inch.

Shape the sideseam of the back through L, I and J towards K as represented. H to N is ¼ bust.

Square down from N. This establishes O, R and S.

By measuring from E to T, we find that for this draft we have 9½ inches, which is 3¼ inches more than the back-waist measure. As the garment is to be made about half-tight through the back-waist, only one-half of the back-waist surplus is taken out as between I and 5, and 3 and 4 as follows:

From I to 5 is one-half of the amount of back-waist surplus to be taken out, say ¾ inch. The remaining ⅞ inch is distributed equally on each side of O as from 3 to 4.

Draw a line from the outer shoulder point of the back through 5 to the bottom. This establishes 10.

From 10 to 8 is ¼ inch. Shape the sidebody through L, 5 and 8 towards V.

Q to Z is 1 inch less than the front hip.

By measuring from Z to 8 and J to 9 we have for this draft 2¼ inches less than one-half of the full hip. This 2¼ inch is distributed equally on each side of R and establishes 6 and 7.

Shape the side-seam of the forepart from N through 3 and 7, and below 7 towards W parallel with the line from 8 to V.

S to X is the same as S to W. Shape the sidebody from N through 4 and 6 towards X as represented.

Any amount may be added forward of the center-of-front line 12, 13, M, Y, as required by the current style, say 2 inches for a single—and 3 inches for a double-breasted front.

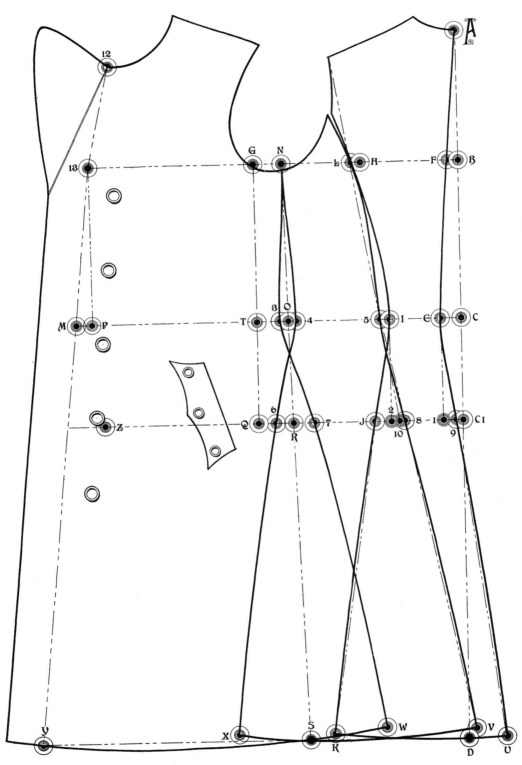

DIAGRAM 87.

THE INVERNESS.

DIAGRAM 88.

THE measures used for the accompanying diagram are for a form of 34 bust, as found on the table of proportionate measures.

TO DRAFT.

Square the lines 1 M and 1 D.

From 1 to A is $\frac{1}{24}$ bust.

A to B is the back-scye depth. A to C is the length to natural waist. A to D is the length. C to C1 is 5½ inches. Square the cross line from B, C, C1 and D.

C to E is ½ inch. Connect A and E. This establishes F.

From 1 to L is ⅛ bust. From 1 to M is the half-back width.

F to 18 is the same as 1 to M. Connect M and 18.

F to G is the blade. Square down from G to establish Q.

G to H is 1 inch more than ⅙ bust. Square up from H.

F to I is one-half of the full bust. I to 13 is ½ inch. Square down from 13 to establish P.

P to 14 is 1 inch. Draw a straight line from 13 through 14 to establish 15.

Draw a straight line from L to I. This establishes 7.

From 7 to 8 is ½ inch. Square down from 18 to establish W.

W to U is 1½ inch. Draw a straight line from 18 through U towards 4, and shape the seam from 8 through 18 and U as represented.

Q to Z is the front hip. C1 to J is 1½ inch.

Draw the center-back seam by a straight line from A through J to K.

J to U and Z to V is 2 inches more than one-half of the full hip. Draw a straight line from 18 through V.

From 18 to S is one-third of the distance from 18 to the waist line. Shape the side-seam below S through V as represented.

G to N is the front-scye depth less the width of the top of the back A to L.

Half-way between A and B establish 5. Connect N and 5.

Connect F and M to establish 3. N to 9 is the same as L to 3.

F to 3 and G through R to 9 is the over-shoulder. In this instance the over-shoulder falls on the line N to 5.

N to 11 is the same as L to 8. Shape the scye from 11 to G as represented by the broken line.

G to 10 is $\frac{1}{16}$ bust. Shape the scye from 9 through 10 to S as represented by the solid line.

N to O is ⅙ bust. Connect O and 13.

(*Continued on page 172.*)

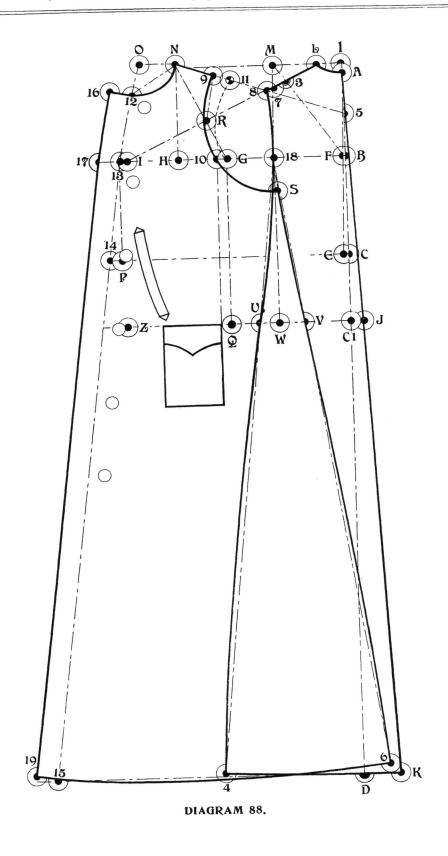

DIAGRAM 88.

N to 12 is ¼ bust.   Shape the neck-gorge as represented.

From 12 to 16, 13 to 17 and 15 to 19 are each 2 inches.

The line from 12 through 13 and 14 is at the center-of-front.   The addition of 2 inches as above forward of this line requires that the button-line be placed 1½ inch back of the center-of-front line.

Pivot at M and sweep forward from midway between D and 4 to establish 4.

From 18 to 6 is the same as 18 to 4.

Pivot at 12 and sweep forward and backward from 15.   Complete the run of the bottom to 6 as represented.

To obtain additional size around the bottom, proceed as explained for Diagram 90.

Square down from 10 to establish the back of the mouth of the pocket.

A hand sling is represented just above the side-pocket extending across the waist-line.

On cutting out the pattern, cut the scye on the line G to 11.   When the cape has been drafted, cut the scye on the line 9, 10, S.

THE CAPE.

DIAGRAM 89.

Lay the pattern of the forepart of the Inverness over another piece of paper.

Mark along the edge of the pattern from 11 towards G, 11 to N, N to 16 and 16 towards 19.   Remove the pattern.

From 16 to 12 and from 19 to 15 are each the same as on the pattern of the forepart.   (Diagram 88.)

N to 1 is the length less the width of the top of the back.

From 11 to 2 is 3 inches.

From 11 to 3 is 1 inch.

Shape the V from 2 to 3, passing ½ inch back of 11.

Lay the pattern of the back of the Inverness in the position shown in broken lines, with the outer shoulder point at 3, and the center-back-seam about square with the front edge of the cape.

Mark along the side of the back from 3 towards 4.

Connect A and 12.

O is half-way between A and 12.

Pivot at O and sweep from 1 towards 4.

From 4 to 5, and 4 to 6 are each 2 inches.

Make notches on the cape and on the back at 5.

From 12 to 7 is ½ inch.

From 15 to 8 is ½ inch.

The line 12 to 15 is the center-of-front.

The line 7 to 8 represents the edge of the fly or top side of the cape.

(*Concluded on page 174.*)

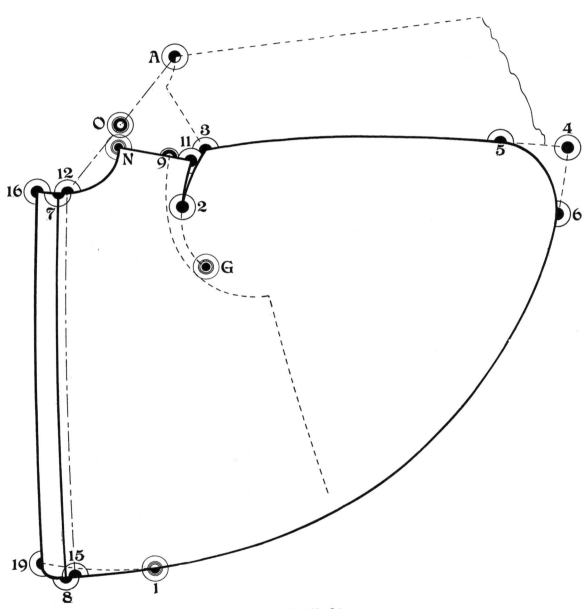

DIAGRAM 89.

The Inverness.

(*Concluded.*)

DIAGRAM 90.

The Inverness has been drafted as explained for Diagram 88, and is represented by the broken line from 1 to 2 and all forward of it.

To obtain additional size about the hips and bottom proceed as follows :

Establish 3 half-way between 10 and S. (Diagram 88.)

Square down from 3 by the bust line to establish 4.

From 4 to 5 is as much as is required.

Mark all along the edge of the pattern forward of the line 3 to 4.

Pivot the pattern at 3 ; swing the lower part back until 4 touches 5, and mark along the edge from 3 to 6 and from 6 to 7.

Reshape from 4 to 7.

It will be found by measuring the pattern of the Inverness on the hip-line from U to J and Z to V (Diagram 88) that there is a surplus of 4 inches over the proportionate size of 40 inches. The additional size given around the bottom as shown on this diagram has also given additional size around the hips, which is represented by the quantity between 8 and 10.

Point 9 is half-way between 8 and 10.

Shape the side-seam from 6 to 7 through 9 or 10 as may be desired.

OPERA CLOAK.

DIAGRAM 91.

THE material represented is a pearl-gray ladies' cloth ; the ornamentation is ermine and chinchilla fur, and the lining is a pale-pink brocaded satin.

The cloak is cut with a box-plaited trained drapery-portion, and a circular yoke that is concealed by a flaring, rippled collarette. The drapery-portion is laid in a wide box-plait at the back-center, one on each side of this plait, another over each shoulder and one at each side of the front. Under the front fold of each front box-plait, just above the waist-line, an opening for the hand may be cut, which will be found convenient when the cloak is closed.

The front edges of the collar and of the front meet flush and are closed with hooks and loops, and the fronts are further finished with jabots of lace-edged chiffon.

A plain cloak can be obtained by omitting the box-plaits. The drapery-portion will then be as is defined by points N, E, O, S, T.

B, L, N, T represents the center-of-back and K, M, O, S, the center-of-front.

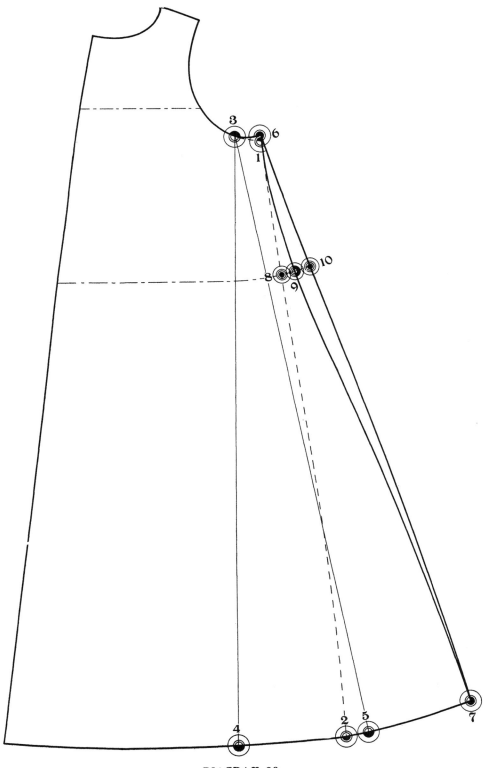

DIAGRAM 90.

TO DRAFT.

Draw a straight line as A H.

A to D is ¼ inch.   Square each way from D.

D to B is ⅛ bust.   Pivot at A and sweep from B.   This establishes C.

C to K is ½ inch.   Shape the neck of the yoke from B to K as represented.

B to I is ¼ bust.   Pivot at D and sweep from I.   This establishes E and J.

I to L is ¼ inch more than ¹⁄₁₆ bust.

J to M is ¹⁄₁₆ bust.   This completes the yoke.

E to F is ¼ inch more than ¼ bust.   F to G is ¼ bust.

Pivot at D and sweep forward and backward from F and from G.

F to N and F to O are each aproximately 1 inch more than ½ bust.   Connect N and O.

N to 2 is one-third of the quantity between E and N.

O to 7 is one-third of the quantity between E and O.

Shape the yoke seam-edge from N through E to O, passing ½ inch below 2 and 7 as represented.   Readjust the length from E to N making it the same as E to L, and that from E to O, making it the same as E to M.

G to P and G to Q are each ⅔ bust.

Draw straight lines from N through P, and from O through Q.

B to L and N to R is round length.

Pivot at D and sweep forward from R.   This establishes H and S.

R to T is 2 inches or more for train.   Reshape from H to T as represented.

This completes the drapery portion for a plain cloak.

THE BOX PLAITS.

Half-way between N and 2 establish 1.

From 2 to 3 is ½ inch less than from N to 2.

From 3 to 4 is the same as from 1 to 2.

From E to 5 is the same as from E to 4.

From 5 to 6 is the same as 3 to 4.

Divide the quantity between H and T into six equal parts.   This establishes 8, 9, 10, 11, and 12.

H to 13 is the same as H to 12.

Divide the quantity between 13 and S into four equal parts.   This establishes 14, 15 and 16.   Connect 1 and 8, 2 and 9, 3 and 11, 4 and 12, 5 and 13, 6 and 14 and 7 and 16.

The shaded portions define the face of the plaits.   The broken lines as from 17 to 18 and on each shaded part, as between 9 and 10, 10 and 11, etc., represent the underfold of the plaits.   All of the underfolds are 3 inches wide at the bottom as from 8 to 17, and ¾ inch wide at the top as from just below 1 to 18.

To produce a pattern for the plaited portion proceed as follows :

Lay the pattern over another piece of paper and mark from 4 to 5 and 12 to 13.   Connect 4 and 12 and 5 and 13.

Add twice the width of the plait, or six inches at the bottom forward of 13, and twice the width at the top or 1½ inch forward of 5.   Draw a line from the top to the bottom and fold the line from 5 to 13 forward until it lies directly over the line just made.   Press the creases flat.

Lay the pattern of the plain cloak on the pattern which is to be plaited and mark from 5 to 6, and from 13 to 14.

DIAGRAM 91.

Add twice the width of the plait, or 6 inches at the bottom forward of 14, and twice the width at the top, or 1½ inch forward of 6. Draw a line from the top to the bottom and fold the line just made backward until it lies directly over the line from 6 to 14. Press the creases flat.

Lay the first pattern over the one which is to be plaited and mark from 6 to 7 and from 14 to 16. Add the same amount as above stated forward of 7 and 16; draw a line from the top to the bottom and fold the line from 7 to 16 forward until it lies directly over the line last made. Lay the first pattern over the one which is to be plaited and mark from 7 to O, O to S and S to 16.

Make the same additions for a plait back of 4 and 12, and fold the line from 4 to 12 backward over the added width. Mark from 4 to 3 and 12 to 11 by the original pattern.

Make the same additions for a plait back of 3 and 11, and fold this part forward over the line 3 to 11. Mark from 3 to 2 and from 11 to 9 by the original pattern.

Make the same additions for a plait back of the line from 2 to 9. Fold the line from 2 to 9 backward over the added width, and mark from 2 to 1 and from 9 to 8 by the original pattern.

Make the same additions for a plait back of the line from 1 to 8. Fold the added width forward over the line from 1 to 8 and mark from 1 to N, N to T and T to 8 by the original pattern.

THE COLLARETTE.

DIAGRAM 92.

Take the yoke pattern which is shown on the preceding diagram and mark all around it. On this diagram it is defined by points B, K, L, M.

Extend the center-of-front and the center-of-back lines until they meet as at A, also down towards E and I. B to E is the back length. Pivot at A and sweep forward. This establishes H. K to I is according to style. In this case K to I is 2 inches more than K to H. Shape the edge to I as represented.

To obtain the ripples proceed as follows : Divide the half-neck B to K into three equal parts to establish C and D. Draw straight lines from A through C and D to establish F and G. E to J is 1 inch. J to 1 and F to 2 are each 1 inch less than half-way between J and F. F to 3, G to 4 and G to 5 are each the same as J to 1. I to 7 is 2 inches and 7 to 6 is the same. Connect B and J, B and 1, C and 2, C and 3, D and 4, D and 5, M and 6, and M and 7.

DIAGRAM 93.

Lay the pattern of the plain collarette over another piece of paper and mark from B to C and J to F. Remove the pattern and connect C and F and B and J.

Points E, J, 1, 2 and 3 are the same as on the preceding diagram. From 3 to G is the same as 3 to F. Connect C and G. J to 4 is the same as J to 1. From 4 to 5 is the same as J to 4. From 5 to H is the same as J to E. Connect B and 5 and B and H. Fold the line C F forward over the line C G. Fold the line B J backward over the line B 5. When thus folded cut across the folds from H to F. Draw a straight line through B and C and square up from B and C.

B to 6 is the height of the collar, 5 inches for this draft. Square across from 6. From 7 to 10 is ½ inch. From 6 to 8 is 1 inch. From 8 to 9 is 1½ inch. Shape the collar from B to 9, and C towards 10 as represented. Cut out the pattern leaving a margin of paper across the top.

DIAGRAM 94.

Lay the plain collarette pattern (Diagram 92) over another piece of paper and mark from C to D, C to F, F to G and D to G. Points 2, 3, 4 and 5 are the same as on Diagram 92.

From 2 to E is the same as 2 to F. Connect C and E. From 5 to H is the same as 5 to G. Connect D and H.

Fold the line C F backward over the line C E. Fold the line D G forward over the line D H. When thus folded cut across the folds from F to G.

Draw a straight line through C and D and square up from C and D.

C to 6 is the same as B to 6 (Diagram 93). Square across from 6. From 6 to 8 is ½ inch. From 7 to 10 is ¼ inch. Shape the collar from C towards 8, and from D towards 10 as represented. Cut out the pattern leaving a margin of paper across the top.

DIAGRAM 95.

Lay the plain collarette pattern over another piece of paper and mark from D to K, D to G, G to I and I to K.

Points 4, 5, 6, 7 and M are the same as on Diagram 92.

From 4 to J is the same as 4 to G. Connect D and J. I to H is the same as I to 6. Connect H and M. Fold the line I M underneath the line from 6 to M. Fold the line D G backward over the line D J. When thus folded cut across the folds from G to H. Draw a straight line through D and K and square up from D.

D to 8 is the same as B to 6 (Diagram 93). From 8 to 9 is ¼ inch. Shape the collar from D towards 9. Cut out the pattern leaving a margin of paper forward of 9 to K.

Lay point 10 (Diagram 94) in a closing position with point 9 (Diagram 95), and point 10 (Diagram 93) in a closing position with point 8 (Diagram 94). Shape the top from 9 to 11 (Diagram 93), 9 to 11 (Diagram 94) and 10 to K (Diagram 95), all as represented.

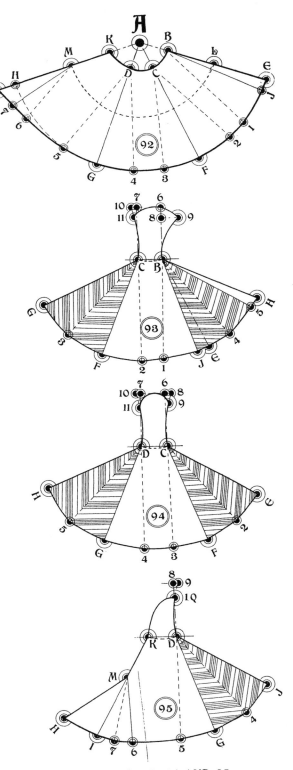

DIAGRAMS 92, 93, 94 AND 95.

ALLOWANCE FOR SEAMS AND INLAYS.

DIAGRAM 96.

THE measures as taken on the form represent the widths and lengths of the finished garment and its parts. As a matter of course, when a pattern has been drafted to the measures without allowance for seams, the allowance must be made elsewhere. It may be made either by cutting each part of the pattern a seam's width outside of the drafting lines, or by first cutting the pattern on the drafting lines, then marking on the material close around the edge of the pattern, and cutting the material a seam's width outside of the chalk mark. Adopt whichever way you prefer.

The question is often raised, " Why are the seams not allowed for on the draft the same as for men's garments?" The answer to this is, " Because of the wide variation in the number of seams in women's garments, different allowances have to be made for each different style which the cutter is called upon to produce."

A woman's coat may be made with one or two bust darts, a sidebody and one or two side forms, or it may have one underarm-seam only. For one extreme fourteen seams must be allowed for as against three for the other.

Another decided advantage in favor of drafting without seam allowance is, that any amount can be added on the material as may be demanded by the fabric, whether closely or loosely woven.

The same applies when cutting skirts. For trousers, knickerbockers, etc., where the number of seams is uniform, the seam and ease allowances may be made on the draft.

On the accompanying diagrams, the material is represented as cut to form the body parts of a tight-fitting garment, with the usual allowances for seams and inlays.

The pattern as drafted to the measures, is defined by the light solid lines.

The seam allowances are represented by the narrow parts lying outside of the light solid lines, as on the side-seam of the back, the back-seam of the sidebody, etc. These are from ¼ to ⅜ inch in width, according to the weave of the material.

Besides this allowance for seams, there should be added inlays as represented by the wider portions lying outside of the lines which define the finished size of each part, as at the front, side and shoulder seams of the forepart, and as represented on each of the remaining parts.

The allowance for seams and inlays should be about as follows :

Add ¾ inch to the center-of-back seam, ¾ inch at the top of the back-scye, and 1 inch at the top of the back.

Add ¾ inch at the top of the sidebody.

Add ¾ inch at the back edge of the underarmpiece.

Add 1 inch at the side-seam of the forepart, the same amount at the front edge, top shoulder, scye, and neck-gorge.

Add 1 inch at the bottom of each part.

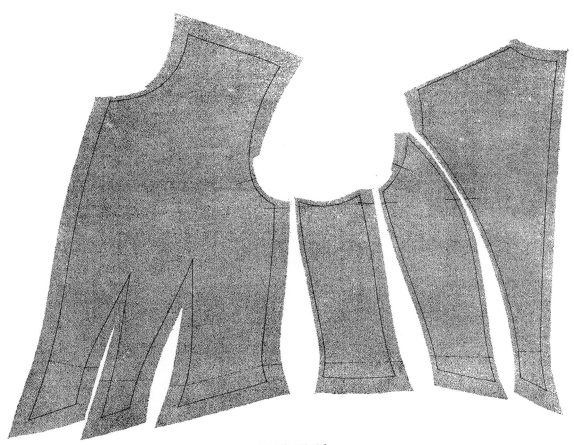

DIAGRAM 96.

The darts should not be cut except as represented.

On all long coats the width of the inlays should be increased below the waist line to 1½ or 2 inches at the bottom of the front edge and side-seam of the forepart, and at the back edges of the underarmpiece and sidebody. The inlays across the bottom of each part should be increased to 2 inches.

Add 1 inch to the forearm seam of the undersleeve, also turn-ups at the bottom of each part 2 inches wide.

The front skirt facings for frock coats should be cut whole with the skirt, so that if required, they may be utilized as inlays.

LAYING OUT.

O N the accompanying diagram is represented the pattern for a two-piece suit laid out ready for marking on the goods. The suit is for a 36 bust size. The skirt is 5 gored and 42 inches in length.

The material is plain faced, has an observable nap, is 4 yards in length and 28 inches in width double fold.

The line A B represents the fold which is laid next to you when the material is to be cut folded in this manner.

Thought must now be given to arranging the several parts of the pattern on the material so as not to use any more of it than is necessary, each part lying *with the nap*, *i.e.*, the top of each towards the right, and the bottom towards the left hand.

As a general rule the largest parts should be distributed on the material first. The smaller parts can then be laid on the spaces between the larger ones. No part should be marked until the positions of all have first been approximately determined.

For the suit represented by this lay-out the largest part, which is the back gore of the skirt, may be laid as represented at the lower end of the material with the front edge in line with the selvage edge, as represented by the line J on the diagram, making allowance for ¾ inch seams on the front and back edges, a ⅜ inch seam at the top, and a facing at the bottom 3 inches wide as represented.

The front edge of the side gore must be laid to run with a lengthwise thread of the material as represented by the line H, making allowances for seams and facing as explained for the back gore.

The center-of-front is usually laid on the crease of the material as represented by the line G, and is cut without a seam on this line. The usual ¾ inch seam should be allowed on the back edge of this gore, a ⅜ inch seam at the top, and a 3 inch facing at the bottom.

This brings the back edges of each of the gores on the bias of the material. When seamed together, each bias back edge is joined to a straight front edge.

For all loose or semi-tight fitting garments, the pattern of the forepart should be laid with the front edge in line with a lengthwise thread of the material as represented.

As the material has a plain face, the remaining parts should be laid to run with the nap, excepting the under-collar, which should always be laid with the front of the sew-on-edge as at K, on a lengthwise thread of the material.

When the material has a decided figure running through it, and the coat is tight fitting, having the usual sideforms, the center-of-back should be laid on a length-wise thread at the top, and 1½ inch or 2 inches forward of the same thread at the waist as represented.

Lay the sidebody so that the seam above C will match the back above D, and the underarmpiece to match the sidebody at the top, as at E and F.

The front edges of the bust darts should be laid to run with a lengthwise thread of the material.

The sleeve should be laid on a lengthwise thread above the elbow.

The front edge of the facing should be laid the same as the front edge of the forepart. They are sometimes (when the material is light weight), made to run through the entire shoulder as represented. More frequently they are made with the back edge extending to the shoulder seam as represented by the broken line.

The back-center of the collar facing should always be laid on the crease-edge, and cut without a seam.

When the material is of a loose weave, or heavy weight, the under-collar should be cut from a light weight melton or some suitable collar cloth of the same color as the material for the coat.

The seam edge at K must not be cut on the bias, but on a lengthwise thread.

Each part must also be so placed on the material as to provide for seams and outlets as represented, and as previously explained.

When the material has an observable nap and a lengthwise figure running through it, or is a plaid, the skirt should be cut circular, i.e., without gores. If it is required that the center-of-front shall be laid on the usual lengthwise fold, then the sides must be pieced out at the selvage edges. Whenever neither the nap nor figure of the material forbids, and it is desired to have the center-of-front on a fold, than the lengthwise fold may be opened out and a cross-fold substituted. This cross-fold may be made as wide as necessary to cut the skirt without piecing.

Mark around each piece with sharply edged chalk. Now cut the material, making the proper allowances for seams and inlays, and notch each part as represented.

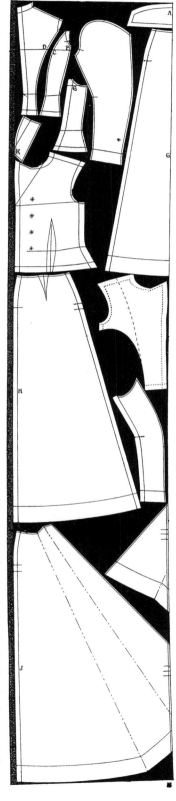

THE TABLE OF PROPORTIONATE MEASURES.

THE proportions of lengths to height, and of widths to bust, vary in different localities. Those which may be correct for one country or section, may not be so for another.

The proportions given in the accompanying table will be found well adapted to general purposes. They are given as a guide to correct measures and as a basis for proportionate patterns.

The student should become familiar with the several lengths and widths, and with their relations to the different heights and bust sizes. This knowledge will serve as a guard against wrong measurements.

To illustrate: The measures for a form of 36 bust and average height will not differ materially from those given on the table. For one who is very erect and has high shoulders, the blade, back-waist and back-scye depth will be less, while the front-scye depth will be more than as given on the table. For one who is stooping and has round and extra sloping shoulders, the blade, back-scye depth and back waist will be more, and the front-scye depth less than as given on the table.

We will suppose that a cutter has taken 10 inches as the blade size of a form of 36 bust. An observation of the form does not show any more prominence or flatness through this part than for an average form and as he knows that the average blade size for this bust is 10 inches, the correctness of the measurement is therefore at once confirmed.

We will also suppose that the measure is either 9¼ or 10¾ inches. If familiar with the proportionate measures the cutter will know at once that, for the first, the form must be very flat, or for the second, very full through the blades, because of the difference between the measurement and the average blade quantity. Should an observation of the form at that part confirm the measurement in either case, all doubt as to its correctness is removed. If it does not, the cutter may know at once that the measure is a false one. He will then re-measure the part until any deviation between the measure and that for an average form is confirmed by the eye, which after some experience can readily detect any flatness or fullness of the form at that part. These observations apply also to all the lengths and widths of all the parts.

In the first column of figures the average heights are given, ranging from 44 inches for a form of 24 bust, to 72 inches for one of 50 bust.

For example take a form 68 inches in height. We find by the quantities placed opposite 68 that the average bust size is 38, back-scye depth 7¼, length from collar seam to the natural waist 15¾, to fork 26½, to knee 41¼, to the floor 58¼, sleeve length 18¼ inches, etc. The difference between the length to the natural waist and the length to the fork gives the anatomical hip-rise, 10¾ inches.

TABLE OF PROPORTIONATE MEASURES.

HEIGHT.	BREAST.	BUST.	WAIST.	HIP.	HALF-BACK WIDTH.	BACK-SCYE DEPTH.	NATURAL WAIST.	COLLAR SEAM TO FORK.	COLLAR SEAM TO KNEE.	COLLAR SEAM TO FLOOR.	BLADE.	FRONT-SCYE DEPTH.	OVER-SHOULDER.	UNDERARM SLEEVE LENGTH.	BACK-WAIST.	FRONT-HIP.	NECK.*	CUFF.*	ELBOW.*
44	24	24	24	25	4¼	5½	11	17⅞	27½	38½	7	8¼	11¼	13	5½	6	11½	7½	10
48	25¾	26	24	28	4½	5¾	11¾	19¼	29¾	41¾	7⅜	8¾	12	14	5½	6½	12	7¾	10
52	27¼	28	24	31	4¾	6	12½	20½	32	45	7¾	9¼	12¾	15	5½	7	12½	7¾	10
56	28¾	30	23½	34	4⅞	6¼	13¼	22	34¼	48¼	8	9¾	13¼	16	5¾	7½	13	8	10¼
58	29½	31	23½	36	5⅛	6⅜	13⅝	22¾	35½	49¾	8⅜	10	13⅝	16½	5¾	7¾	13¼	8	10¼
60	30¼	32	23½	38	5¼	6½	14	23½	36½	51½	8¾	10¼	13⅞	16¾	5¾	8	13½	8¼	10½
62	31½	33	23	39	5½	6⅝	14⅜	24¼	38	53½	9	10½	14¼	17	5¾	8¼	13¾	8½	10¾
64	32¾	34	23	40	5⅝	6¾	14¾	24¾	38¾	54¾	9⅜	10¾	14⅝	17¼	5¾	8½	14	8½	11
65	33½	35	24	41	5⅞	6⅞	15	25⅛	39½	55¾	9¾	11	14⅞	17½	6	8¾	14¼	8¾	11¼
66	34¼	36	25	42	6	7	15¼	25½	40	56½	10	11¼	15¼	17¾	6¼	9	14⅝	9	11½
67	35	37	26	43	6⅛	7⅛	15½	26	40¾	57½	10¼	11½	15⅝	18	6½	9¼	15	9	11¾
68	36	38	27	44	6¼	7¼	15¾	26½	41¼	58¼	10½	11¾	15⅞	18¼	6¾	9½	15¼	9¼	12
	37	39	28	45	6½	7¼	15⅞				10¾	12	16¼	18¼	7	9¾	15⅝	9¼	12¼
69	38	40	29	46	6⅝	7⅜	16	26¾	42	59¼	11	12¼	16⅝	18½	7¼	10	16	9½	12½
	39	41	30	47	6¾	7⅜	16⅛				11¼	12½	16⅞	18½	7½	10¼	16¼	9½	12¾
70	40	42	31	48	7	7½	16¼	27	42½	60	11⅝	12¾	17¼	18½	7¾	10½	16⅝	9½	13
	41	43	32	49	7⅛	7½	16¼				11⅞	13	17½	18¾	8	10¾	17	9¾	13¼
	42	44	33	50	7¼	7⅝	16⅜				12¼	13¼	17¾	18¾	8¼	11	17¼	9¾	13½
	43	45	34	51	7⅜	7⅝	16⅜				12½	13½	18	18¾	8½	11¼	17⅝	9¾	13¾
71	44	46	35	52	7⅝	7¾	16½	27½	43¼	61	12⅞	13¾	18¼	19	8¾	11½	18	10	14
	45	47	36	53	7¾	7¾	16½				13⅛	14	18½	19	9	11¾	18¼	10	14¼
	46	48	37	54	8	7⅞	16⅝				13½	14¼	18¾	19	9¼	12	18⅝	10¼	14½
	47	49	38	55	8⅛	7⅞	16⅝				13¾	14½	19	19	9½	12¼	19	10¼	14¾
72	48	50	39	56	8¼	8	16¾	28	43¾	61¾	14⅛	14¾	19¼	19¼	9¾	12½	19¼	10½	15

* These are jacket sizes.

When drafting add 1 inch to the hip-rise for ease. The difference between the natural waist length and the floor length gives the front length for a skirt, 42½ inches. The difference between the fork length and the floor length gives the length of leg, 31¾ inches.

Corresponding lengths for any height given on the table can be obtained in the same manner.

For stout, fleshy forms, the back-scye depth and hip-rise will be more, and the length of the leg will be less, than as given on the table.

The half-back widths, and the size of sleeves at the cuff and at the elbow as given on the table are correct for the present time, but are subject to changes in style.

A cutter may be called upon to draft a pattern from a few fundamental measures as bust, waist, hip and height. In such cases the height is as important as any of the other measures mentioned. Without it the proper lengths of the whole and of its parts cannot be determined. The lengths may vary materially from those which accompany a given bust size, because the form may be of a different height than that given on the table for that bust size.

For example: Take a form of 38 inches bust and 66 inches height. The widths for the half-back and blade would be the same as they are given in the row of figures in which 38 bust is found. The back-waist would be the same as given in the row of figures in which the required size of the waist is found. The front-hip would be the same as given in the row of figures in which the required hip size is found.

The lengths would be as they are given in the row of figures in which 66 is found as the height, which are 7 back-scye depth, 15¼ length from collar-seam to the natural waist, 25½ to fork, 40 to knee, 56½ to floor, 17¾ sleeve.

The front-scye depth and the over-shoulder should each be shortened the same amount as the back-scye depth. This will give 11½ front-scye depth and 15⅝ over-shoulder for a form of 38 bust and 66 inches in height.

All of the lengths and widths of the parts are subject to other modifications as will be suggested by a description of the form which should always accompany orders of this kind, as "stands erect, normal or stooping," "blades flat, normal or full," "shoulders high, normal or extra sloping," etc.